FENCES & GATES

By the Editors of Sunset Books

Sunset Books
Director, Sales & Marketing: Richard A. Smeby
Production Director: Lory Day
Editorial Director: Bob Doyle

Sunset Publishing Corporation
Chairman: Jim Nelson
President/Chief Executive Officer: Stephen J. Seabolt
Chief Financial Officer: James E. Mitchell
Publisher: Anthony P. Glaves
Circulation Director: Robert I. Gursha
Director of Finance: Larry Diamond
Vice President, Manufacturing: Lorinda B. Reichert
Editor, Sunset Magazine: William R. Marken

Fences & Gates was produced in conjunction with
St. Remy Press
President/Chief Executive Officer: Fernand Lecoq
President/Chief Operating Officer: Pierre Léveillé
Vice President, Finance: Natalie Watanabe
Managing Editor: Carolyn Jackson
Managing Art Director: Diane Denoncourt
Production Manager: Michelle Turbide

Editorial staff for *Fences & Gates*
Senior Editor: Heather Mills
Editor: Marc Cassini
Assistant Editor: Jennifer Ormston
Senior Art Director: Francine Lemieux
Art Director: Normand Boudreault

Book Consultant
Don Vandervort

Special Contributors
Eric Beaulieu, Michel Blais, Robert Chartier, François
Daxhelet, Hélène Dion, Jean-Guy Doiron, Lorraine Doré,
Dominique Gagné, Michel Giguère, Christine M. Jacobs,
Solange Laberge, François Longpré, Joan Page McKenna,
Geneviève Monette, Jacques Perrault, Rebecca Smollett,
Judy Yelon

COVER: Landscape Architect: Susan Edwards Ogle,
Landscape Design. Builder: James B. Green, Jr., General
Building Contractor. Photography by Philip Harvey. Photo
Direction by JoAnn Masaoka Van Atta. Cover Design by
Kevin Freeland.

Third printing April 1998

ISBN 0-376-01106-8
Library of Congress Catalog Card Number: 95-070329
Printed in the United States

For additional copies of *Fences & Gates* or any other Sunset
book, call 1-800-526-5111.

Acknowledgments
Thanks to the following:
American Hardboard Association, Palatine, IL
American Homeowners Foundation, Arlington, VA
American Permahedge, Richmond Hill, NY
American Technocrete Corporation, Los Angeles, CA
American Wood Preservers Association, Woodstock, MD
American Wood Preservers Institute, Vienna, VA
Bufftech, Buffalo, NY
City of Stockton Permit Center, Stockton, CA
Coastal Lumber Company, Uniontown, PA
Forest Products Laboratory, U.S. Department of Agriculture
  (Forest Service), Madison, WI
Heritage Vinyl Products, Assumption, IL
Home Depot, Providence, RI
Idaho Cedar Sales, Inc., Troy, ID
International Fence Industry Association,
  Stone Mountain, GA
Maze Nails, Peru, IL
Giles Miller-Mead, Brome, Que.
Omega Fence Systems Inc., Laval, Que.
Protect-A-Child Pool Fence Systems, Inc.,
  Pompano Beach, FL
Seymour Manufacturing Co., Inc., Seymour, IN
Stanley Door Systems, Troy, MI
Walpole Woodworkers, Inc., Walpole, ME
Watertown Bureau of Code Enforcement, Watertown, NY
Western Wood Products Association, Portland, OR
Wynntech Distribution Inc., Laval, Que.

Picture Credits
p. 4   courtesy Walpole Woodworkers, Inc.
p. 5   *(upper)* Jack McDowell
p. 5   *(lower)* courtesy Idaho Cedar Sales, Inc.
p. 6   *(both)* Ells Marugg
p. 7   *(both)* courtesy Walpole Woodworkers, Inc.
p. 8   *(upper)* Ells Marugg
p. 8   *(lower)* courtesy Walpole Woodworkers, Inc.
p. 9   *(upper)* courtesy Walpole Woodworkers, Inc.
p. 9   *(lower)* Jack McDowell
p. 10   *(upper)* Ells Marugg
p. 10   *(lower)* Steve W. Marley
p. 11   *(upper)* Steve W. Marley
p. 11   *(lower)* Ells Marugg
p. 12   courtesy Heritage Vinyl Products
p. 13   *(upper)* courtesy Bufftech
p. 13   *(lower)* courtesy Protect-A-Child Pool Fence
        Systems, Inc.
p. 14   courtesy Walpole Woodworkers, Inc.
p. 15   *(upper)* courtesy American Permahedge
p. 15   *(lower)* courtesy Omega Fence Systems, Inc.
p. 16   *(upper)* courtesy American Technocrete Corporation
p. 16   *(lower)* Robyn Shotwell

CONTENTS

FENCE AND GATE CHOICES

Fences and outdoor screens can transform a yard into a secure, attractive retreat from the outside world. When well designed, they filter the sun's glare, transform a biting wind into a pleasant breeze, and help mute the cacophony of street traffic, noisy neighbors, and barking dogs. As partitions, they divide the yard into separate areas for recreation, relaxation, gardening, and storage.

In this chapter, you'll find photographs of fences made of wood, vinyl, different types of metal, glass, and even concrete. The fences, gates, and screens that you'll learn how to build in this book are constructed mainly of wood, although much of the information—including design considerations as well as layout and construction details—applies to other types of fences. However, the specific construction details for other fence materials differ significantly from one manufacturer to another, so if you want to install a fence that isn't made of wood, be sure to follow the installation instructions that come with the product you buy.

Your fence and gate should harmonize with the architectural style of your house. Using pickets of different lengths, this fence creates a scallop effect that complements the trim details on the house.

WOOD

Many fences are built partly or entirely of wood. The versatility of wood as a fencing material is reflected in the wide variety of its forms—split rails, grapestakes, dimension lumber, poles, and manufactured wood products like plywood and tempered hardboard.

On the following pages, you'll find photographs of a number of wood fences, gates, and screens—from rustic post-and-rail fences to more formal designs like the lattice screen. A fence will also support espaliered plants or serve as a backdrop for creative garden lighting effects.

This post-and-rail fence covers a lot of ground with a minimum of wood. The rails are 10 feet long, with tapered ends that fit through the mortised posts.

This split-rail fence, made of split red cedar, borders a yard without blocking the view the way a more solid fence might. Cedar's natural properties protect it against decay.

Not all post-and-rail fences are rustic; the more formal style shown here uses 2x6 lumber for the rails along with 4x4 posts. Painted white for appearance and weather protection, this fence would be at home just about anywhere.

The arrowhead-shaped tops of these posts and pickets impart a distinctive look to this fence. Specially designed pickets and posts like these can be shaped by a homeowner or cut at a cabinet shop.

The curved corner section of this picket fence gives a personalized touch to a traditional style—and also provides a perfect spot for growing flowers.

Different fence materials, such as these wood pickets and stone pillars, can be combined to create distinctive fence designs.

This tall, stepped-down board fence with lattice top is paired with a matching gate to protect a city yard on a busy hillside street. The gaps at the bottom are filled by brick footings. (Design: James McLean)

The curving lines of the arch-topped picket gate provide visual contrast to the right angles of this board fence and lattice top.

This fence looks the same from both sides, which is likely to please the neighbors. Since the boards are staggered on opposite sides of the rails, there is more air circulation through the fence than if the boards were all attached on the same side.

Attached to a pool house, this louver screen gives swimmers both privacy and shelter from the wind. (Design: Gene Kunit)

Flowing gracefully down a steep hillside lot, this fence of narrow grape-stakes easily follows the contour of the land. (Design: Gene Kunit)

This heavy-duty lattice fence is made primarily of 2x2s. An opening for the tree—a mature white oak—enables the fence to blend in with its surroundings creatively. (Design: Richard Schadt)

This board-and-batten fence provides an ideal background for uplighting of trees and plants. (Lighting design: Epifanio Juarez Design)

Carefully trained ivy adorns this 6-foot-high grapestake fence. Maintaining this espalier takes time, but the results are striking. (Design: Jack Stafford)

VINYL

Vinyl fencing is available in many of the same styles as traditional wood fencing: post-and-rail, post-and-board, picket, and various board fence styles. Vinyl fences are usually easy for the average do-it-yourselfer to install, but the specific installation details vary, depending on the manufacturer and the style of fence.

Many of the tools and some of the tasks for installing a vinyl fence are the same as for a wood fence. For example, in either case you'll have to plot a straight fence line and dig the postholes. But the next steps—setting the posts and attaching rails and siding—will depend on the specific fence you're installing. Unlike typical wood fence construction, for vinyl fences it's not always recommended to set all the posts first and then go back to install the rails. For certain vinyl picket fences, for example, the bottom rail is inserted between posts before the

posts are set in concrete, then the pickets are inserted in the bottom rail, and finally the top rail is installed. In any case, follow the instructions that come with the product you buy.

Once installed, vinyl fences are easy to maintain: They won't rust or peel, and since the color is integral to the vinyl, they don't need painting. Since vinyl doesn't take paint well, choose a color you like.

Vinyl is also used in fences for more specialized purposes, such as the pool security fence shown opposite. This safety fence is designed to keep children and nonswimmers away from the pool itself while still permitting access to the pool area. This removable barrier requires more specialized installation techniques; it is recommended that you have a professional handle the job.

This vinyl picket fence and gate will withstand the elements without needing regular maintenance. A pair of cane bolts attached to the gate posts slide into holes in the ground to keep the gate closed.

Many styles of wood fencing are also available in vinyl; this basketweave fence is similar to the wood basketweave fence shown on page 70.

This vinyl-mesh pool fence only encloses the pool, enabling children to play in the pool area safely. The fence can be removed easily to provide access to the pool.

FENCE AND GATE CHOICES **13**

OTHER FENCE AND GATE MATERIALS

Next to wood, wire is perhaps the most versatile fencing material. Wire for exterior use is made of galvanized steel and may be coated with polyester or vinyl; it's available in a number of gauges (or thicknesses), mesh sizes, and roll lengths and widths.

Wire fences, including chain link, are useful for providing security, supporting plants and vines, enclosing play yards and animal pens, and protecting garden areas from small animals. Welded or woven mesh and chain link can be attached to a wood framework or they can be installed as part of an all-metal fence.

Extruded-plastic fencing, which is usually a mesh resembling wire fencing, can be used in many of the same applications as wire or chain-link fences; it can even sometimes be fastened to poles from an existing wire fence.

Ornamental metal fencing used to mean ornamental iron—those elegant wrought-iron masterpieces that graced the mansions of the Victorian era. Today, the term encompasses not only traditional wrought iron, but ornamental steel and aluminum as well. Designs in all three metals range from ornate hand-crafted works

of art to sleek modern grillwork available in prefabricated sections. There are contractors who specialize in the installation of ornamental metal fences, because the job is somewhat complex. Or, you can install prefabricated sections yourself.

Although we usually associate masonry materials—brick, stone, and concrete—with walls rather than fences, some of these materials do have applications in fencing. But building masonry walls or screens requires specialized masonry techniques, so consult a contractor.

Fences and outdoor screens made of glass or plastic can block wind around small patio areas without blocking views or sunlight. In larger areas, glass and plastic, like any solid barrier, are relatively ineffective in blocking wind. In small areas exposed to the weather, glass is more suitable than plastic because of its high resistance to abrasion.

If you're considering a glass fence or screen, get professional assistance. The supporting structure must be rigid so that the glass cannot be twisted, which causes breakage; it must also be designed to accommodate the expansion and contraction of the glass.

Ornamental metal fencing may be made of aluminum, traditional wrought iron, or steel, like the fence shown here. Steel and aluminum require significantly less maintenance than wrought iron, since they don't rust and seldom need to be painted.

Designed to give a fence the look of a closely trimmed hedge, these wire and PVC inserts make a chain-link fence more solid, providing greater privacy.

This attractive steel mesh fence provides security with style. The color is baked on, so the fence never needs painting.

Although this fence looks as though it consists of individual bricks mortared together, it is actually made of concrete panels. Installation is well within the skills of the average do-it-yourselfer and the finished fence is essentially maintenance-free.

This glass wind screen shelters a hillside patio area without sacrificing the panoramic view of the hills beyond. The screen was designed for standard-size glass door panels. (Design: Ortha Zebroski)

PLANNING AND DESIGN

The planning and design stage is perhaps the most important part of a fence-building project. You'll need to decide what you want the fence to do: provide security or privacy, direct foot traffic through the yard, or give protection from the sun and wind, for example. You'll also need to decide whether you require a fence or an outdoor screen. Outdoor screens are simply sections of fence, either freestanding or acting as partial walls around patios, decks, and other outdoor spaces. They serve many of the same functions as a tall fence—providing privacy, blocking unwanted views, or alleviating wind and sun problems.

An outdoor screen becomes a fence when it encloses a large section of property, such as a backyard. The other difference between fences and screens is that fences usually require gates. You can design your gate to blend in unobtrusively with the fence, or to contrast with it in style or building material.

In this chapter, we'll guide you through the steps in planning a successful project. You'll need to think about the fence's intended purpose and where you want it to go. Consider what type of fence best fits the surrounding landscape and architecture and what materials will be used to build it. Finally, determine whether the fence will meet local codes and ordinances, who will design and build it, and how much it will cost.

In the design section, you'll find information on drawing plans and dealing with obstacles; a good way to assess your needs is to make a scale drawing of your site *(page 23)*. The materials you choose for your fence or gate will affect both the look and the cost of your project. Beginning on page 29, we'll show you how to choose building materials for your fence. Building materials and hardware for gates are discussed beginning on page 34.

In this chapter, you'll learn how to adapt your fence to the existing landscape—to avoid a tree, as shown, or to follow the curve of a hill.

FENCE BASICS

On the opposite page, several common styles of fences are illustrated. These can be varied for the particular look you want; some other possibilities are shown beginning on page 59.

Fences serve many more functions than a simple demarcation of your lot's border. Below and on page 20 you'll find out just what a fence can do to improve your property. As you're planning your fence, keep these factors in mind, then read page 21 to make sure your fence ideas are in line with local regulations.

Fencing for security: In the broadest sense of the term, security fencing includes any fence designed to keep people in or out of a designated area; it should be tall, sturdy, and hard to climb. Many fence designs fit this description; the most popular are those using vertical boards, plywood panels, heavy-gauge wire mesh, or chain link. Psychology plays an important part in the design of a good security fence. For example, a solid board or panel fence may be a more effective psychological deterrent than a chain-link fence, simply because it's impossible to see what's on the other side.

Security fencing can contain children within an area such as a play yard. A childproof fence should be high and sturdy and should provide no toeholds. Small wire mesh (2x2) is ideal for play yards—its open design allows parents to keep an eye on their children's activities, but the small holes make it hard to climb over.

Many communities require fences around swimming pools to protect children and nonswimmers. But even if there's no such ordinance in your area, installing fences around your pool area is a good idea. Make sure your design meets local code requirements. You can also buy removable vinyl fencing to enclose just the pool itself so that children can play safely in the pool area.

Containing animals: In rural areas, fences are required to keep livestock from straying and ruining neighbors' crops. Suburbanites who move to the country and wish to keep a few horses, chickens, or other livestock on their property need to know about these fence types. Though most weekend farmers don't have to worry about enclosing miles of land, the requirements for containing animals still apply.

Pet owners, too, are responsible for their animals. If you keep a dog on your property, you'll want to give special consideration to the fence design. Though few dogs can climb or jump a 6-foot fence, most can dig under one, and large dogs can break through a flimsy wood fence. Chain link, heavy wire, or solid panels set in a ribbon of concrete will prevent dogs from gnawing through or digging underneath. Metal fencing is preferable to wood because it is not damaged by scratching and gnawing.

Screening for privacy: The most effective privacy fences and screens are those you can't see over, under,

around, or through. But you'll want to give some forethought to the design and location to avoid the feeling of a boxed-in space. You can break the monotony of a solid barrier by changing the face treatment of alternating sections (for example, the size or direction of boards and the color of panels).

A series of high-and-low or open-and-closed sections can block unwanted views (and peering neighbors) while preserving desirable sights beyond the yard. For instance, you can use solid sections where you want to block the line of sight, and open sections of transparent glass or plastic, wire, or spaced boards or pickets where you want a view. A louver fence can be very effective in blocking a view while allowing air circulation within the yard. Placed horizontally, louvers will shut out a view completely; placed vertically, they allow only a small section of the yard to be seen by anyone walking along the fence line.

Defining outdoor spaces: In a yard, fences and screens can delineate areas for work, recreation, relaxation, storage, and gardens. Low or open fences can physically separate areas while visually preserving the overall size of the yard. You can use taller screens to hide unattractive sights, such as trash or service areas, work centers, or swimming pool equipment. Where added security is required, choose chain-link fencing with solid inserts woven into the chain link.

Tempering wind, sun, and noise: A fence or screen can effectively control the elements of wind and sun to create a pleasant environment in your yard. To achieve this, the first thing you'll have to do is study how the sun and wind affect your property at various times of the year; then plan fence design and location accordingly. Outside noise, too, can be reduced by solid fences and screens.

As a rule, a solid barrier provides little wind protection across large expanses of yard—the wind simply vaults over it and continues at the same velocity a few feet downwind of the barrier. Tests have shown, though, that a wind screen or fence with an open design (spaced boards or slats, louvers, or woven lath) breaks up a steady wind into a series of eddies or small breezes. Compared with the effect of a solid fence, this action protects a larger area behind the fence or wind screen from the main force of the wind. The drawings on page 20 show the effects that several fence designs have on the wind, and relative temperatures at various distances beyond the fence.

Fences and screens can be designed to admit full sunlight, provide partial shade, or admit no sun at all on their shady sides. Transparent glass or plastic screens admit the maximum amount of light and a clear view while offering wind protection around patios and decks.

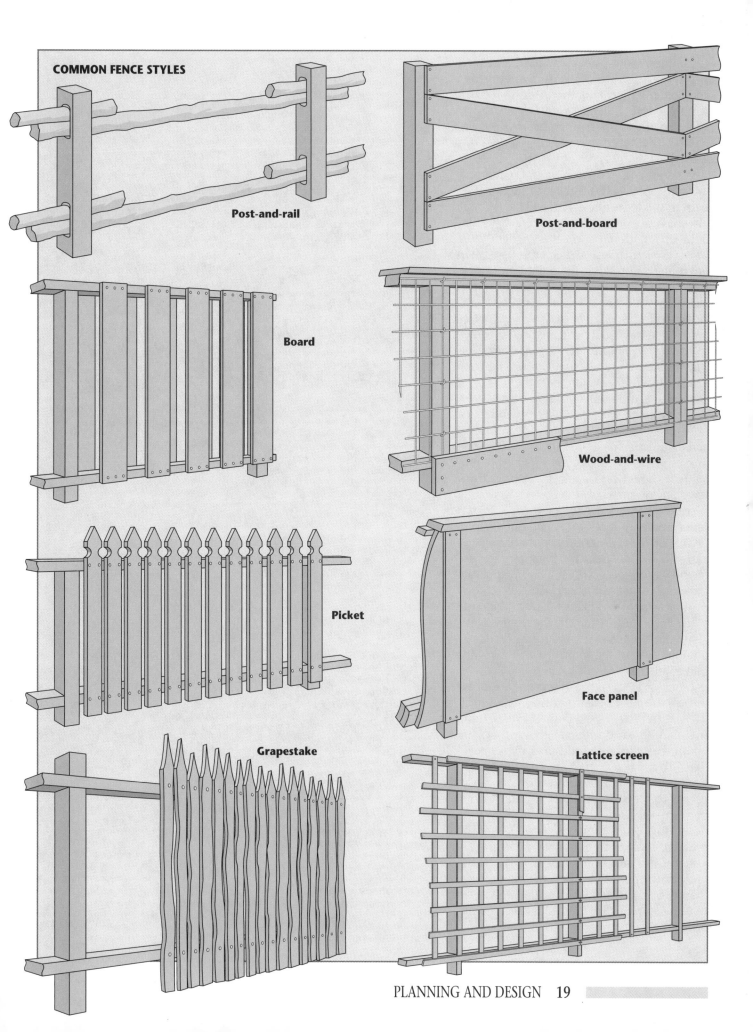

COMMON FENCE STYLES

Post-and-rail

Post-and-board

Board

Wood-and-wire

Picket

Face panel

Grapestake

Lattice screen

You can reduce heat and glare from the sun by using tinted or glare-reducing glass or plastic, which cuts the intensity of the sun's rays, yet allows a view beyond. Latticework or other open designs provide partial or filtered shade, necessary for the growth of many types of plants.

When it comes to muting noise, one rule always applies—the thicker or higher the barrier, the more effective it will be. It should also have a solid, unbroken surface; joints between boards or panels must be tight-fitting or covered with lath strips. Of course, there are practical limits to the height and thickness of a fence or outdoor screen (a solid masonry wall actually works best of all in cutting off noise). But there is a psychological advantage in visually cutting off the source of the noise: Though the actual noise level may be reduced only slightly by a fence or screen, it will seem quieter if the source of the noise is hidden from view.

Landscaping with fences: Plants and fences go together naturally. Fences and outdoor screens can be designed to support vines and espaliers (shrubs or trees trained to grow against the fence) or to act as a backdrop for planting beds. In turn, carefully selected plants can soften the stark expanse of a bare fence and add depth to its two-dimensional character. The color and texture of a fence can also complement the color and texture of the plantings against it when you plan a harmonious relationship. Dark fences contrast pleasingly with light foliage and blooms. With light-colored fences, the reverse is true —an example is the traditional, striking combination of red roses backed by a white picket fence.

Fences and screens can serve as a support or backdrop for other planting structures, such as trellises, raised planter boxes, hanging planters, or potting sheds. Or they can be used as climate modifiers in your garden—to break a prevailing wind or to cast shade in areas where you want shade-loving plants to grow. Plan the type and location of your plantings at the same time you're designing a new fence or screen. Keep the fence in scale with existing landscaping, and choose new plantings that will be in scale with the fence when they grow to mature size and shape. More detailed information on planting around fences begins on page 84.

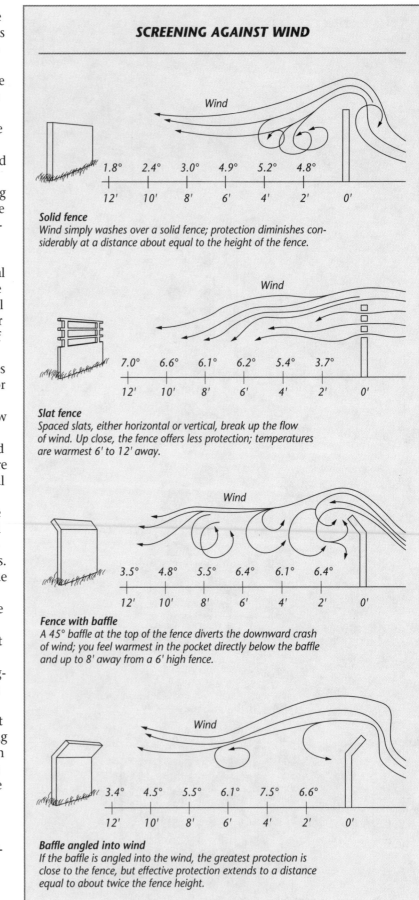

SCREENING AGAINST WIND

Solid fence
Wind simply washes over a solid fence; protection diminishes considerably at a distance about equal to the height of the fence.

Slat fence
Spaced slats, either horizontal or vertical, break up the flow of wind. Up close, the fence offers less protection; temperatures are warmest 6' to 12' away.

Fence with baffle
A 45° baffle at the top of the fence diverts the downward crash of wind; you feel warmest in the pocket directly below the baffle and up to 8' away from a 6' high fence.

Baffle angled into wind
If the baffle is angled into the wind, the greatest protection is close to the fence, but effective protection extends to a distance equal to about twice the fence height.

Before you make any specific plans for the size, design, and location of your fence or outdoor screen, look into the local codes and ordinances that may influence these decisions. Requirements and restrictions will vary considerably from state to state, city to city, and even neighborhood to neighborhood.

There are regulations covering many different fencing situations. Restrictions on barbed wire, electric fencing, glass, and other materials of a hazardous nature are almost universal. And there are various ordinances limiting the height of fences around yards, and fences situated near traffic intersections. In addition to height restrictions, there are likely to be code-imposed setback distances from buildings, property lines, or the street that will affect the intended location of your fence or screen.

Fence height: Most communities have height restrictions on boundary or division fencing. Although these restrictions may vary from one community to the next, front-yard fencing is generally limited to 4 feet in height, and backyard fencing is generally limited to between 6 feet and 8 feet. Some communities allow the standard fence height to be exceeded if the extended portion is composed of wire mesh, lattice, or other open work.

Fences that border intersections or sharp bends in the street must meet certain height restrictions and setback distances from the street to allow motorists an unobstructed view of oncoming traffic.

In all such matters, though, never assume—always check with local authorities about fence height and setback distances. If your plans do conflict with local regulations, you may be able to obtain a special permit.

Use of hazardous materials: Using any fence material intended to cut, impale, or otherwise injure is restricted in most residential communities. Most local codes are fairly specific on hazardous materials and their uses. Materials such as barbed wire and electrified fencing are usually restricted to farm, commercial, and industrial uses. Glass used in fencing must be tempered glass rather than ordinary window glass.

Boundary and division fences: From the time the first fence was built to define a property line, such barriers have provoked many a dispute, both in and out of court. Even if the fence is built to resolve land ownership disagreement, problems can arise concerning fence ownership and maintenance. To help minimize these and other potential conflicts, it's wise to make a written agreement with your present neighbors concerning fence design and location; if possible, try to enlist their active cooperation in building the fence.

If you're building a fence directly on the property line, make a written agreement with the adjoining landowner(s) in advance, specifying location and type of fence, and dividing the responsibility for building and maintaining it. If possible, have the agreement recorded at the city or county clerk's office to avoid future ownership disputes, should either of the properties change hands. If built on the property line, the fence belongs both to you and to the adjoining landowners, though they are under no obligation to help build it, pay for it, or even maintain it, unless that written agreement has been made. The neighbors' only obligation is to refrain from defacing or destroying the fence intentionally—and this, of course, doesn't take into account poor taste in colors, should the neighbors decide to paint their side.

It may not always be possible to get your neighbors' cooperation. One solution to this problem is to build the fence at least 6 inches in from your side of the property line. That way, you don't need to consult the neighbors on its construction or maintenance, since fences are generally considered to belong to the land on which they're built. To avoid ownership disputes, you'll need an accurate survey of the boundary to be sure the fence is correctly placed. But this method offers no assurance that your neighbors won't resent the fence, or you for building it. Building a fence that looks as good on the neighbors' side as on your side is one way to help avoid ill feelings.

Required fencing: Fence laws and codes not only restrict and regulate the type of fence you can build, but may even require you to erect a fence in certain instances. For example, many communities require protective fences to enclose swimming pools or to contain livestock or pets, as discussed on page 18. Open wells, excavations, and other potentially dangerous features on your property may also require fencing.

Sources of information: The most obvious source of information on fence codes and restrictions is your local building department or community planning office. Fence contractors are also familiar with local codes and building practices and apply them in their work. It's important not to make assumptions or to rely on information given by neighbors. For example, it's not safe to assume that your proposed fence is appropriate just because it is similar to existing fences in the neighborhood—new zoning ordinances may have been passed since the older fences were built. In such cases, the new regulations will apply to your situation. Always seek advice from local authorities before erecting any fence or outdoor screen.

DESIGNING YOUR FENCE

Once you've chosen a suitable type of fence and have roughly determined its location on your property, it's time to plan the details.

The overall appearance of your fence will depend not only on the basic style you've chosen but also on the materials used in its construction, its actual dimensions (height, post spacing, material dimensions), and the characteristics of the property on which it sits. All of these design elements must harmonize to form a functional and attractive structure.

With careful planning, you can save on materials without sacrificing quality. Some designs that use fewer materials than others may be perfectly adequate for your needs. You may also be able to use an economically priced type of siding with good results. Depending on the complexity of your project, you might save money in the long run by hiring a professional to design the fence. For information on working with professionals, turn to page 28.

For information on working with professionals, turn to page 28.

PLAY IT SAFE

BEWARE OF UNDERGROUND OBSTACLES
Before you dig, get your local utility companies to indicate where any underground cables or pipes cross your property; you may need to alter your plans to avoid them.

MAKING PLANS

Fence projects, large and small, should be fully planned, either on paper or on a computer, before you start building. This will allow you to conceptualize the entire project in advance and experiment with various ideas. In addition to helping you estimate materials, the drawings will enable you to visualize the effect the fence will have on the overall landscaping scheme.

Your first design consideration will be the actual site on which the fence is to be built. Be sure to take into account lot size, shape, and grade, sun orientation, wind direction, and the characteristics of surrounding structures and plantings. You should also plan your fence to harmonize with the architectural style of your house.

The best way to learn more about your property is to obtain a plot or site plan, if you don't already have one. Architects' drawings often include an overall site plan along with the house plans; here you'll find the lot size, shape, and grade along with the house size and location. If your house was designed by an architect, you can get these plans from the architect; if not, try the developer or the contractor who built the house, or possibly a previous owner. If the property was professionally landscaped, the landscape architect who did the work should be able to supply you with a detailed site plan showing planting locations on the lot. You can get deed maps showing the actual dimensions and orientation of the site from your city hall or county courthouse, from the title company, or from the bank putting out the loan on the house.

The first step in drawing up your plans is to make an accurate scale drawing of the property, or of the portion of the property where the fence or screen will go. You'll then need an accurate drawing of a section or two of the fence itself. Keep in mind that you can save money and avoid wasting material if you design your fence to make the best use of standard lumber lengths, which are generally in multiples of 2 feet. For instance, posts spaced 4, 6, or 8 feet on center— the distance from the center of one post to the center of the next—make the best use of the pieces that run across the posts, such as rails and kickboards. To avoid waste and unnecessary cutting of siding materials, round off fence height to the nearest foot.

ASK A PRO

HOW CAN I SKIRT A BANK?
When a fence has to be built along the edge of a bank, bluff, or cliff, it's a good idea to enlist the aid of a landscape architect or an engineer; either will be able to tell you just how close to the edge the fence can be without eventually being lost to erosion. Posts must generally be sunk deeper than usual to accommodate shifting soil. Plantings along the bank may be able check soil erosion, but in some cases a retaining wall will be necessary. Many municipalities require a permit for any retaining wall, so be sure to consult your local building department.

To build a fence on top of a retaining wall, the posts can be fastened to the masonry with post anchors.

Use your site plan as a guide and make your scale drawing on a large sheet of 1/4-inch graph paper; a sample scale drawing is shown below. Make your drawing a workable size: Use a scale of 1/8 or 1/16 inch = 1 foot. Include the following features: the overall dimensions of the lot, the location of the house and other existing structures, the direction of north and of the prevailing wind, the path of the sun, easements and setback distances from buildings, property lines, and the street (available from your local building department), existing plantings, and any problems off the lot that may affect sun, view, or privacy.

Once your lot drawing is complete, lay a sheet of tracing paper over it and sketch various fence ideas. If the fence is part of an overall landscaping project, include the sizes and locations of proposed plantings and structures. When you've come up with an idea you're satisfied with, make a detailed drawing of the fence layout by itself on a tracing paper overlay.

Next, make an accurate elevation drawing of one or two sections of fence to help you visualize your design and estimate quantities of materials later. Your drawing should show post spacing, sizes of lumber or other fence material, and overall dimensions of posts, rails, and siding. The drawing directly below is an example of an elevation drawing for a board fence. For some other fence designs, see page 19.

Elevation drawing
*Helps you visualize design
and estimate materials.*

Scale drawing of site
*Use to plan location and
determine function of fences
and outdoor screens.*

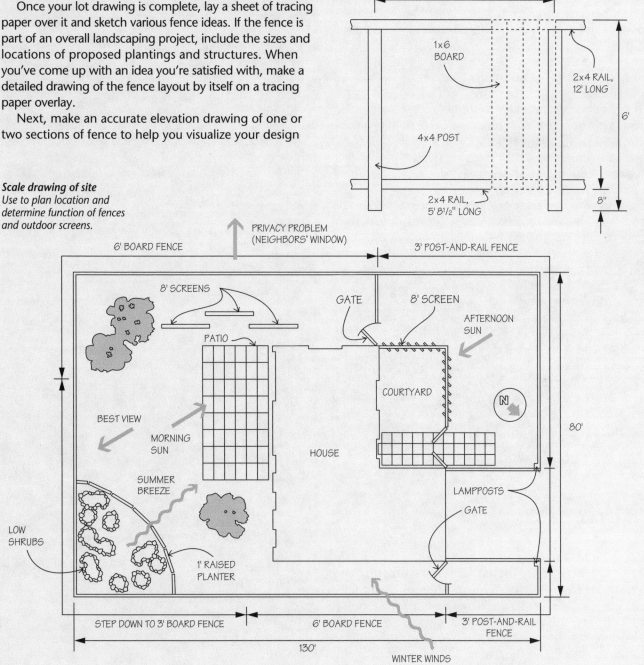

LAYOUT PROBLEMS

If every lot were free of obstructions, as smooth as a well-maintained baseball diamond, and measured in even increments of 6 feet, laying out a fence over its surface would be very simple. But often the fence planner must figure out how to get the fence around a tree or curve, up a slope, or across a ditch or depression.

Climbing hills: If your fence line runs uphill, there are two basic ways you can lay out the fence: one is to follow the natural contours of the land; the other is to lay out the fence in steps. The method you use depends on both the basic design and the fence materials.

Some designs that adapt especially well to contour fencing are post-and-rail fences, and solid fences using pickets, palings, or grapestakes. Stepped fences, more geometric in form, are more difficult to design and build, but they are a good solution for board, louver, basket-weave, and panel fences. The illustrations at right show examples of contour and stepped fencing.

In either stepped or contoured fencing, the bottoms of boards 6 inches or wider should be cut to follow the contour of the hillside, as the close-up drawings below show; otherwise, triangular gaps will result where the fence siding meets the ground, giving the fence an unfinished look and providing animals easier access. For tips on plotting hillside fences, see page 41.

Dealing with obstacles: Sometimes fence layout can be complicated by one or more trees growing in the path of the fence line. You have three alternatives: You can make

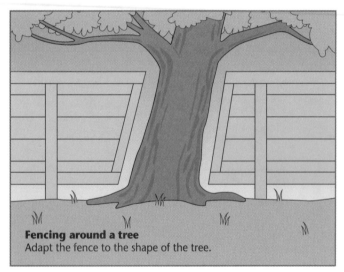

Fencing around a tree
Adapt the fence to the shape of the tree.

the tree part of the fence, relocate the fence, or remove the tree. To incorporate the tree into the fence, install posts several feet from either side of the trunk (so that no damage is done to the tree's root system) and extend the fence to within a few inches of the trunk, as shown in the drawing above. The ends of the fence should be far enough away from the tree to allow the contour of the trunk to change over the years.

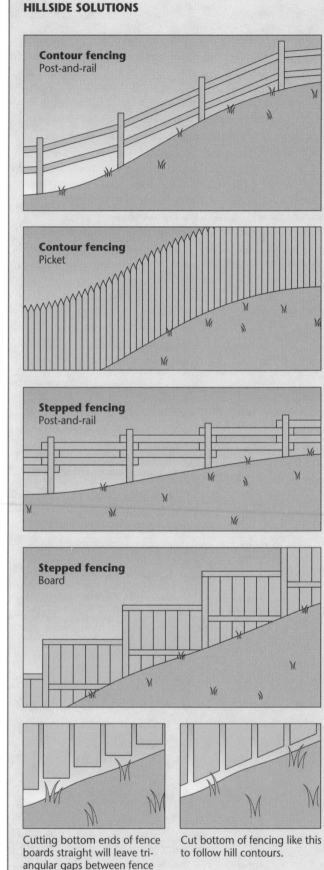

HILLSIDE SOLUTIONS

Contour fencing
Post-and-rail

Contour fencing
Picket

Stepped fencing
Post-and-rail

Stepped fencing
Board

Cutting bottom ends of fence boards straight will leave triangular gaps between fence and hill.

Cut bottom of fencing like this to follow hill contours.

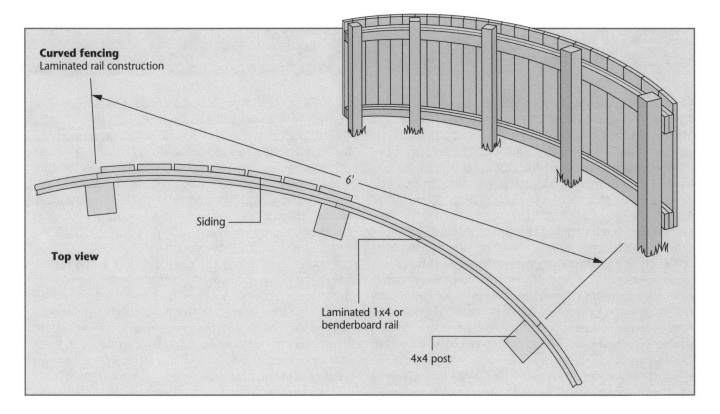

Curved fencing
Laminated rail construction

Top view

Siding

6'

Laminated 1x4 or
benderboard rail

4x4 post

Don't attach the fence to the tree in any way—nails or screws driven into the trunk allow bacteria and disease to enter. Similarly, wire or other materials wrapped around the trunk would eventually restrict the flow of sap, injuring or killing the tree.

You may also need to adjust your fence to avoid a large rock or fill a depression. Running a fence over a rock is similar to fencing around a tree: Shorten the fencing above the rock to follow the contour of the rock and add horizontal framing to support the truncated boards. To span a hole, extend boards into it below the bottom rail, adding a rail to support the longer fencing, if necessary.

Making curves: There are two ways to design a curved fence—along a true arc or in short, straight sections angled to form an arc. To secure a true arc, you can make the top and bottom rails curved by laminating pieces of benderboard or, for a shallow arc, pieces of decay-resistant 1x4 lumber *(above)*. The other choice is to bring the fence around in a series of short chords or sections; this works best for designs using panels *(below)*. Instructions for plotting a curved fence are on page 40.

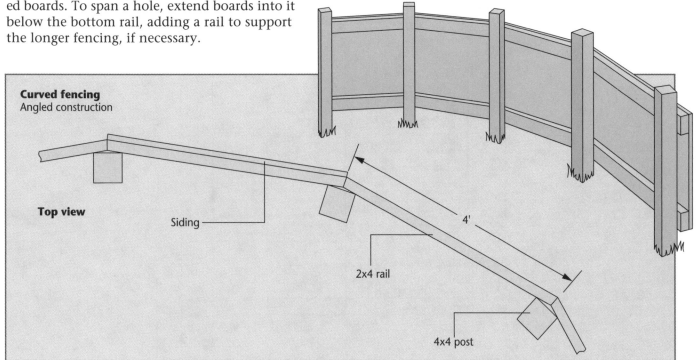

Curved fencing
Angled construction

Top view

Siding

4'

2x4 rail

4x4 post

DESIGNING YOUR GATE

If your fence plan includes a gate, you'll need to decide where the gate will go, and how it will be designed. Remember that gates get more wear and abuse than any other part of a fence or wall. To last, gates must be solidly built and attached with top-quality, heavy-duty hardware. A number of attractive gate designs can be found in the color section beginning on page 4; instructions for building a gate start on page 53.

Choosing the location: Deciding where to locate your gate is usually fairly simple—gates are located for convenience. For example, a gate will be needed where a fence intersects a walk or driveway. Study your present yard layout, giving consideration to proposed additions or changes that may affect traffic patterns. Then decide where the gate or gates best fit into the fence line. In new landscaping, gate locations are dictated by the overall landscape plan.

Selecting a style: Your own taste is your best guide to a gate design you can live with. Your choice, though, should be influenced by the styles of surrounding structures, particularly the fence or wall in which the gate will be set. For example, an ornamental iron gate may accent a brick wall perfectly but would look quite out of place in a rustic split-rail fence.

Gates can either match a fence or contrast with it. Inconspicuous gates are sometimes built for security reasons, but more often because an obtrusive design would cause an unattractive break in the fence line.

Conversely, a gate can be designed to call attention to itself in order to lead visitors to the proper entrance. Front entry gates are often showpieces, reflecting the artistic tastes of their owners.

Because the latch is the device people reach for to open and close the gate, it is often the focal point of the gate design. So it's a good idea to consider carefully the appearance as well as the mechanical operation of the latch. Not all latches are suitable for every gate. You must either choose a latch that works with your gate design or, if you've found a latch that suits your fancy, adapt the gate design to work with the latch.

Determining size: Once you've decided on the location and basic design, you'll need to consider what size the gate will be so you can determine post size, spacing, and location. The dimensions of your gate will depend

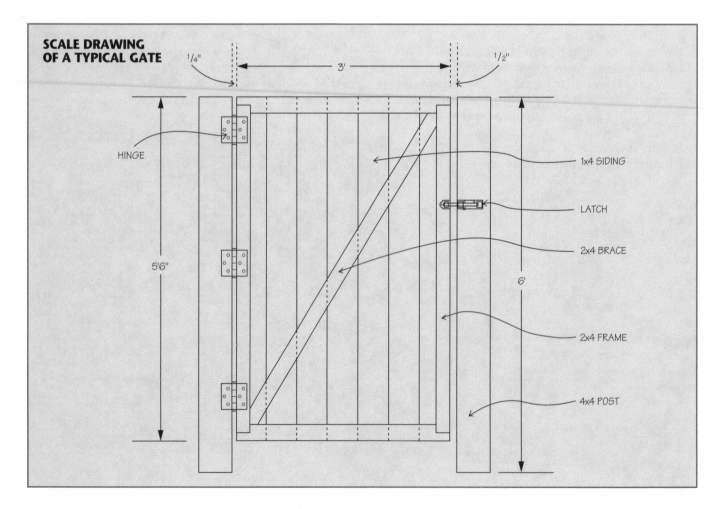

SCALE DRAWING
OF A TYPICAL GATE

1/4"   3'   1/2"

HINGE

1x4 SIDING

LATCH

2x4 BRACE

5'6"   6'

2x4 FRAME

4x4 POST

on the height of the fence it serves, and the width of the walk, path, or driveway it must span. When figuring the width of the gate opening, think about the type of traffic that must pass through it.

Walk-through gates should provide adequate clearance for yard maintenance equipment (such as wheelbarrows and garden tractors), garden furniture, and other large items that are periodically moved through the entry. Driveway gates should provide clearance for trucks as well as for cars. A possible solution for wide openings is a double gate, especially if your design calls for solid, heavy gate construction.

Opening your gate: Your gate can either swing or slide open. Commonly used for driveways, sliding gates operate on either wheels or rollers attached to a track set in the ground. A few types are suspended on an overhead track, but these are usually not suitable for driveways because of the low overhead clearance. Your other option is a swinging gate, either double or single. Swinging gates are discussed at right.

You may want to install an electric gate operator. On driveway gates, these are installed for both security and convenience. Similar in principle to the electric garage door opener, gate operators can be operated by a switch in the house (often in conjunction with a two-way intercom), a keyed switch or keypad outside the gate, remote controls inside a car, or a combination of these. Models are available for single and double swinging gates and sliding gates. Electric locking devices can also be installed on walk-through gates, so house occupants can be selective about visitors. You'll find electric gate operators in the Yellow Pages under "Door Operating Devices."

PUTTING PLANS ON PAPER

Once you've planned your gate—style, location, size, basic materials, and types of hardware—make a detailed drawing of it. This will help you in ordering materials and building the gate. A typical drawing is shown opposite.

Your drawing should include the overall dimensions of the gate itself, the height of gate posts and distance between them, and the dimensions of individual framing and siding pieces. You should also indicate the clearance space between the gate and the gate posts on both the latch and hinge sides ($3/4$ inch total is standard), and the position of the latch, the hinges, and other hardware.

GATE SWING OPTIONS

Your choice of the direction in which a gate swings will be influenced by both the location of the gate and the design of the fence or wall on which it's hung. Entry gates usually swing inward toward the house or driveway; likewise, gates in boundary fences swing into your property. A gate on your property can swing in the direction of greater traffic flow. On sloped ground, hang the gate to swing toward the downhill side so it can easily clear the ground. Gates with very wide posts, such as those set in masonry walls, are usually centered and can be hinged to swing in either direction. Or, you can align the gate with one side of the posts or the other. In any case, you'll require enough of a gap on the latch side to allow the gate to clear the post.

For safety, a gate that adjoins stairs should be placed at the top of a flight of steps, and should swing away from the steps. This way, pedestrians will have to stop to open the gate and become aware of the steps. The illustrations below show other gate situations.

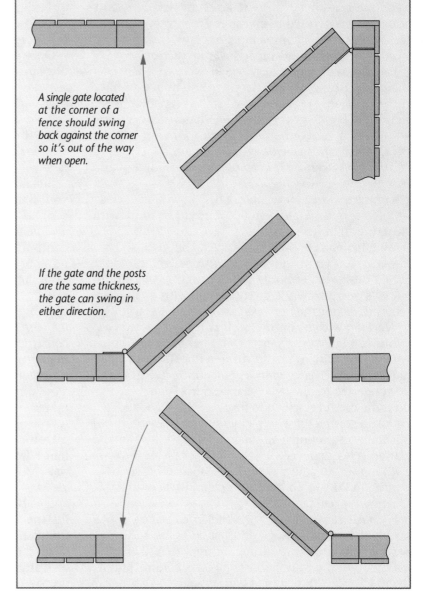

A single gate located at the corner of a fence should swing back against the corner so it's out of the way when open.

If the gate and the posts are the same thickness, the gate can swing in either direction.

BEFORE YOU BEGIN

If you need assistance in designing your fence, there are several ways to go about it. The most complete and unified design is likely to come from a landscape architect or landscape designer, who will plan the whole garden scheme with the fence integral to it. This, of course, is usually the most expensive way to go and is generally only necessary if you are engaging in a major landscaping project.

Choosing a landscape architect, designer or contractor: If you merely need advice on specific designing problems, you can work with a landscape architect or designer on a per-hour consultation basis. In some cases, you may want to have a set of plans drawn up, for a specified fee.

Landscape architects are state-licensed professionals with a degree in landscape architecture. They're trained in both the aesthetics and the structural details of landscape design. If hired to do the entire project, the architect will provide a complete set of plans, negotiate bids from contractors, and supervise construction.

Landscape designers have varied experience and training in landscape design. They're not required to have the state license of a landscape architect, which means that there are no government regulations concerning who can call him or herself a landscape designer. However, many landscape designers do have a landscape contractor's license and can provide both design and installation services.

Contractors are also capable of helping you with design problems, but their experience tends to be more with structure than with aesthetics.

Whether you choose a landscape architect, a landscape designer, or a contractor to help with design or to do the actual design and building, first examine the professional's previous work; be concerned with quality and whether or not the person's tastes parallel your own.

Working with a contractor: If you decide to have a contractor build your fence, you'll naturally want one who does quality work and guarantees it. Unless you've had prior experience with a good contractor or have been referred to one by a reliable source, you'll have to do some careful research to find one. It's a good idea to choose a contractor who's a member of one of the various trade associations. Although membership in an association is no guarantee of reliability, it at least implies a willingness to comply with the association's code of ethics. And if you do have a problem, there is an organization you can turn to.

For a list of association members in your area, contact one of these trade associations, such as the National Association of the Remodeling Industry (NARI) at 1-800-440-NARI or the National Association of Home Builders Remodelors™ Council in Washington, DC. Or you can contact the American Homeowners Foundation in Arlington, Virginia.

Usually, it's best to discuss your project with more than one contractor. Be as precise as possible about what you want, and write down any questions you have. Your choice should be based on the individual's reputation as a fence builder rather than simply the lowest bid, although a low bid doesn't necessarily mean inferior work. You'll want a contractor who's cooperative, competent, and financially secure; check bank and credit references. Reputable licensed contractors are also insured for property damage, public liability, and workers' compensation, for their own legal protection and yours.

The contractors' estimates should include a complete list of materials and price breakdowns; it's best to get a fixed-price bid. The contractor may reserve the right to withdraw the estimate, after an agreed-upon period, if the bid is not accepted.

Once you've chosen a contractor, the next step is to draw up a solid contract that includes detailed drawings and descriptions of all work to be done, a description of materials to be used (lumber species and grades, hardware and fasteners, finishes, and so forth), a time schedule, a firm price, and terms of payment. You can buy a sample contractor agreement, written in straightforward language, from the American Homeowners Foundation.

Building it yourself: If you intend to design and build your fence yourself, you may want to use one of the computer software programs available for drawing plans and sketching ideas. You can buy these programs at computer software dealers. If you don't have a computer at home, you may be able to use one at your local public library.

Fence building is not technically difficult, but the work is often physically demanding. For this reason, it's wise to have someone work with you on the actual construction, especially when you're setting and aligning fence posts. Ask a friend or neighbor to help, or hire a laborer when needed. The first step will be to acquire a building permit, if one is required. Then make your materials list and begin shopping for materials; the following section will help you select them.

Don't overlook the wide variety of prefabricated fence designs in wood, vinyl, metals, and other materials. Most manufacturers of prefabricated fencing provide brochures and other information on the various applications of their fencing, along with installation instructions. Prefabricated fencing can be obtained from fence dealers, lumber suppliers, and home centers, or directly from the manufacturer. Actual building techniques for fences start on page 37 and for gates on page 53.

FENCE MATERIALS

Rough estimates made early in your planning will help you to compare overall costs of various fence designs, but more detailed estimates are needed for ordering materials. Base your calculations on your completed scale drawings of the fence *(page 23)* and gate *(page 26)*, if your fence plan includes one.

No matter which building materials you choose for posts, rails, and siding, you'll need fasteners—nails, screws, bolts, or brackets—to put them all together. Concrete mix, too, will be on your shopping list, as the posts of most fences should be set in concrete. If you intend to apply a finish, order finishing materials—paint, stain, or clear finish. The information on the following pages will help you estimate the quantities of lumber and other materials you'll require.

Once you have your materials list, you're ready to order. If possible, hand-pick all lumber from your building supplier or lumberyard. If your fence project is very large, you may prefer to place an order through a lumberyard and have the lumber delivered. In either case, it's best to visit several suppliers to compare prices and inspect lumber quality before you buy—if you simply order by phone and have the lumber delivered sight unseen, you may end up with inferior-quality lumber. Try to get competitive bids on the total amount of lumber and other materials you'll be buying.

LUMBER

Lumber used in fences is usually dimension lumber —wood surfaced to a specific thickness and width. A number of sizes and grades of lumber are suitable for fencing. Most wood fences use 4x4 posts and 2x4 rails; for extra strength you can use 6x6 posts. Lumber used for siding can be pickets, lath, or boards in various sizes, either rough or surfaced. To extend the life of your fence, you'll want to use a decay-resistant wood species or lumber that's been pressure-treated with a wood preservative. Other important considerations in choosing lumber are surface texture, moisture content, actual lumber dimensions, and overall lumber quality. On the following pages, we'll tell you what to look for in selecting lumber.

For a rustic-looking fence, you can use split wood— rough split rails, grapestakes, or poles. Split wood poles come in various sizes, from 3 inches to 12 inches or larger in diameter. You can buy them either smooth-turned on a lathe to specific diameters, or in the rough —cut from saplings with bark and branches removed. Six-inch-diameter poles are most commonly used as fence posts; they're available pressure-treated with a preservative for that purpose. Smaller-diameter poles, often called palings, are used for stockade-type fencing.

You can also use resawn lumber—made from thicker planks sliced down the middle—for a rustic look; it's rough-textured, but not splintery. Resawn lumber is dried, not green, and generally somewhat more expensive than rough lumber.

DECAY-RESISTANT LUMBER
Wood fence members that come in contact with the ground are more susceptible to decay and termite attack than above-ground portions of the fence. Unless lumber is treated with a wood preservative or is cut from the heartwood of a decay-resistant species *(page 31)*, it will last only two or three years underground before becoming structurally unstable.

Pressure-treated lumber: Pressure-treating is a commercial process whereby a preservative is forced deeply into the wood. Fence members treated in this manner will last up to 50 years below ground. Pressure-treated woods have superior decay resistance over woods that have been simply dipped or soaked in a preservative.

Preservatives most commonly used in the pressure-treating process are inorganic arsenates such as chromated copper arsenate (CCA) and ammoniacal copper arsenate (ACA), dissolved in water and other solvents. One drawback to these woods is their color: The chemicals leave a greenish-brown tinge to the wood. They can, however, be painted or stained. Pentachlorophenol and

PLAY IT SAFE

HANDLING PRESSURE-TREATED LUMBER
The different types of pressure-treated lumber require different safety precautions. Inorganic arsenical pressure-treated wood, which is what you're most likely to find at a lumberyard, should never be cut indoors and should never be burned; dispose of it with ordinary household trash or bury it. When cutting this type of lumber, wear respiratory protection (a dust mask or respirator) and safety goggles.

The other types of pressure-treated lumber, which you're more likely to find as used lumber (such as old railway ties) require added safety precautions. Never burn this type of lumber, always cut it outside, and wear safety goggles, respiratory protection, long pants and a long-sleeved shirt, and chemical-resistant vinyl-coated gloves when handling it.

creosote are also used to pressure-treat wood, but not generally in residential applications.

When buying pressure-treated lumber, look for the stamp that indicates compliance with the American Wood Preservers Association (AWPA) standards governing both the quantity of chemical in the wood and its depth of penetration. Wood that is labeled "treated to refusal" does not necessarily comply with the AWPA

MANUFACTURED PANELS (SHEET PRODUCTS)

An old standby for solid panel fences and screens, exterior-grade plywood comes in standard 4x8 sheets, although sheets up to 10 feet long are also available. Plywood is also used as a backing for wood and masonry siding materials. Thicknesses range from 3/8 inch to over 1 inch; the most common sizes used for fencing are 3/8 inch, 1/2 inch, 5/8 inch, and 3/4 inch. Surface texture can be smooth, rough-sawn, or grooved. You can buy plywood unfinished, primed for painting, or prestained in a variety of colors.

Plywood panels under 3/4 inch thick require extra framing for support; the fence should be framed like a wall in your house. For panels 3/8 inch thick or less, attach 2x4 vertical studs to the top and bottom rails and space them 16 inches on center. For panels 1/2 to 5/8 inch thick, space the 2x4s 24 inches on center. Panels 3/4 inch or thicker require no extra framing, but their weight makes it necessary to use sturdier posts and rails in the fence design.

Hardboard is made of wood fibers, rendered from chips of waste wood, that are bonded with adhesives under heat and pressure. Hardboard comes in standard 4x8 sheets, in thicknesses from 1/8 inch to 1/4 inch. It's fairly heavy and quite strong—relatively thin panels can be used for fencing. Hardboard may be smooth on one side and textured on the other or smooth on both sides. It can be painted easily, but its medium to dark brown surface won't take a stain. If properly painted, it offers good resistance to weather and won't crack or split under normal conditions. For either type of hardboard, choosing a durable finish (paint or stain) is important in helping to prevent moisture damage. Like most paneling materials, hardboard needs studs (vertical supports) between top and bottom rails to prevent bowing. Hardboard is fairly easy to cut, but it dulls standard tools quickly; use carbide-tipped blades. Pilot holes should always be drilled for fasteners.

You can buy house siding made from either plywood or hardboard; install it as you would siding on your house. You'll have to paint the back and all edges, and, unless you buy siding that's pretreated with water repellent, the front surface as well. NOTE: Some hardboard siding is prefinished and comes with a 25-year guarantee.

COMMON LUMBER DEFECTS TO WATCH OUT FOR

Knots
Although knots are primarily visual defects, large, loose ones in posts and rails can weaken a fence; loose or dead knots—surrounded by a dark ring—are more likely to fall out than are knots intergrown with surrounding wood (called watertight knots).

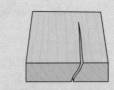

Split
Crack extending through entire thickness of board, often at the ends.

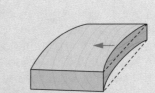

Crook
Warp along the edge of a board from end to end; also known as crown. Caused by incorrect seasoning.

Bow
Warp along the face of a board from end to end; caused by improper storage.

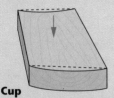

Cup
Hollow across the face of a board; minor cupping can be corrected when nailing.

Check
Crack along the length of a board not passing through the entire thickness of the wood; badly checked ends should be cut off before boards are used.

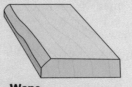

Wane
Missing wood along the edge or corner of a board cut from the outside of a log; posts and rails with this defect may be difficult to nail, resulting in weak joints.

Decay
Caused by microorganisms that attack moist or wet wood; treat decayed areas with a water sealer before using the lumber.

standards. It has been treated with chemicals to the point where it won't take any more—but that point may be below the AWPA standard. With wood labeled in this way, there is no guarantee that the level of chemical penetration is sufficient.

Use pressure-treated lumber on all fence members up to 6 inches above ground level. Any cuts in pressure-treated wood should be treated with a commercially available wood preservative containing copper naphthenate.

Decay-resistant species: Some woods have a natural resistance to decay and termite attack. Available species include redwood and red cedar. Only the heartwood (darker colored wood toward the tree's center) of these species has this resistance and can be used for fence members in contact with the ground. This all-heart lumber will last 5 to 10 years or more underground, depending on soil moisture conditions. Though not as resistant as pressure-treated lumber, this wood may be your choice for reasons of cost, availability, or aesthetics.

All-heart lumber is usually more expensive than grades containing both heartwood and the lighter colored sapwood. One way to cut fencing costs is to select posts from the less expensive grades that contain at least 3 feet of solid heartwood at one end, so only the heartwood portion will come in contact with the ground. Remember that the sapwood of a decay-resistant species will not resist decay.

LUMBER GRADES

After lumber is cut from logs, it is sorted and graded according to wood species, quality, moisture content, and eventual use. To ensure uniform quality from the many independent lumber mills across the country, manufacturers' associations have developed grading standards for each of the commercial wood species. Graded lumber is either identified with a stamp or inventoried by grade before being shipped to the lumberyard.

Generally, lumber grading depends on natural growth characteristics, on defects resulting from milling errors, and on manufacturing techniques in drying and preserving that affect the strength, durability, or appearance of each board. But these mill-assigned grades only partially indicate the quality of the lumber you're buying. Often, lumberyards and home improvement centers will re-sort and re-designate mill-graded lumber to suit their operations. Redwood, especially, tends to be called whatever the lumber dealer thinks will sell: supreme, deluxe, economy, decking, fence boards, or garden grade.

Unless the pieces are stamped with a grading mark, it's hard to tell which grade you're getting. Also, the quality of lumber differs from one yard to the next, depending on damage from shipping, how the lumber is stacked, and how long it's been sitting there. So it's important to develop an eye for sound lumber and to hand-select each piece, if possible. Common lumber defects that affect the appearance and strength of wood—and your fence—are shown opposite. Learn to spot these defects right at the lumberyard.

Aside from grading based on natural defects and milling imperfections, lumber is sorted according to surface texture and moisture content.

UNSEASONED, KILN-DRIED, OR AIR-DRIED LUMBER

Most lumber is dried, either kiln dried or air dried in stacks, before it is considered ready for use. It is then marked according to its moisture content: unseasoned or green lumber with a moisture content of 20% or higher is marked S-GRN; lumber with a moisture content of 19% or less is labeled S-DRY; and lumber dried to 15% or less moisture content is marked MC-15. The moisture content of lumber dramatically affects shrinkage, nail holding, and other important properties of wood; the greater its moisture content, the more likely it is to split, warp, or cup as it dries. Although you can build serviceable fences and gates with green lumber, usually S-DRY lumber is the best option.

NOMINAL AND SURFACED SIZES

Logs are cut into lumber at the mill and the dimensions of these rough-cut boards (the nominal sizes) are then used to identify them: A 2x4 in its rough state is 2 inches thick by 4 inches wide.

Most lumber is dried, though, and as a result, it shrinks slightly; some of it is then planed for surface quality, which reduces it to its surfaced size. So the 2x4 you get when you order dry, surfaced lumber actually measures $1\frac{1}{2}$ inches by $3\frac{1}{2}$ inches.

When buying rough lumber, you'll find the actual dimensions will be closer to the nominal ones, depending on the moisture content of the wood and on cutting tolerances allowed by the mill where it's been sawn. The chart below shows the nominal and surfaced sizes of

STANDARD DIMENSIONS OF SOFTWOODS	
Nominal size	Surfaced (actual) size
1x2	$\frac{3}{4}$"x$1\frac{1}{2}$"
1x3	$\frac{3}{4}$"x$2\frac{1}{2}$"
1x4	$\frac{3}{4}$"x$3\frac{1}{2}$"
1x6	$\frac{3}{4}$"x$5\frac{1}{2}$"
1x8	$\frac{3}{4}$"x$7\frac{1}{4}$"
1x10	$\frac{3}{4}$"x$9\frac{1}{4}$"
2x4	$1\frac{1}{2}$"x$3\frac{1}{2}$"
2x6	$1\frac{1}{2}$"x$5\frac{1}{2}$"
2x8	$1\frac{1}{2}$"x$7\frac{1}{4}$"
4x4	$3\frac{1}{2}$"x$3\frac{1}{2}$"
6x6	$5\frac{1}{2}$"x$5\frac{1}{2}$"
6x8	$5\frac{1}{2}$"x$7\frac{1}{4}$"

standard softwood lumber. Lath and pickets or boards under 1 inch in thickness or width are identified by their exact size.

APPEARANCE

Rough or unsurfaced lumber can give the fence a rustic quality, but remember that a rough surface is difficult to paint with a brush or roller, and is likely to leave splinters in the hands of anyone who touches it. (Resawn wood is available in some lumberyards; it's rough textured but not splintery.) For a more finished appearance, choose surfaced lumber. It's easier to paint or stain, though somewhat more expensive per board foot than rough lumber. To save money, you could use rough lumber for posts and rails, and surfaced lumber for siding.

TIPS ON SELECTING LUMBER

When choosing your lumber, check each board for defects. Many lumberyards will allow you to dig through the piles as long as you keep them neat. The top pieces on the pile are usually the undesirable "flops"—those rejected by other buyers because they are damaged, discolored, or becoming deformed as they dry. So look deeper—wear heavy gloves and bring along a helper when sorting through the pile.

To check for twisting, warping, and cupping *(page 30)*, hold up each board and sight down its length. Boards with long, slow curves are much easier to straighten when nailing than those with tight little crooks. When selecting lumber for posts and rails, try to avoid "bull's-eye" pieces milled from the center of the log—they tend to crack and warp more than other pieces.

ESTIMATING LUMBER NEEDS

Estimating lumber for a fence or an outdoor screen is primarily a matter of measuring and counting up the number of pieces needed for construction. The most economical fence designs use standard lumber lengths, which keep cutting and waste to a minimum. But if your design requires odd-size pieces, determine the most economical way to cut them from available lumber lengths; lumber is generally sold in multiples of 2 feet. For instance, if you need 4½-foot-long boards, you can cut four of them from an 18-foot-long board with no waste, rather than cutting them from a 6-foot, 10-foot, or 14-foot-long board with unusable short pieces left over. You can reduce your lumber costs even further by ordering the most readily available, suitable species and the lowest grade of lumber for your needs. You'll find it easier to make intelligent choices by looking at the lumber that is available in local lumberyards.

To estimate, first count the number of posts in your plan and determine their lengths. The post length includes the post height (above ground) and the post depth (below ground). To determine how deep posts should be set, see page 42. Next, determine the total amount of material needed for rails and siding. Using your elevation drawing as a guide *(page 23)*, determine the number and lengths of pieces needed to build one section of fence, then multiply this amount by the total number of sections. If the sections are of unequal lengths, rails and siding will have to be figured separately for each section. Finally, add 10% to the total amount of both rail and siding materials to allow for waste and building errors.

FENCE HARDWARE

Before ordering your lumber, estimate the quantity of nails and other hardware you'll be using. Most lumberyards and building suppliers either carry or can order virtually everything you'll need, so having a complete materials list on hand will save you extra trips. First determine the types and sizes of nails your fence will require, then the quantities you'll need. Since you'll be using many nails, it'll be cheaper to buy them in bulk.

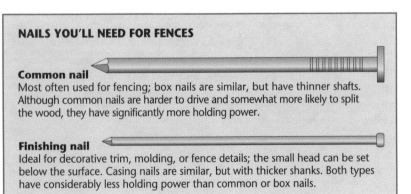

NAILS YOU'LL NEED FOR FENCES

Common nail
Most often used for fencing; box nails are similar, but have thinner shafts. Although common nails are harder to drive and somewhat more likely to split the wood, they have significantly more holding power.

Finishing nail
Ideal for decorative trim, molding, or fence details; the small head can be set below the surface. Casing nails are similar, but with thicker shanks. Both types have considerably less holding power than common or box nails.

COMMON NAIL SIZES	
Size	Length
2d	1"
3d	1¼"
4d	1½"
5d	1¾"
6d	2"
7d	2¼"
8d	2½"
9d	2¾"
10d	3"
12d	3¼"
16d	3½"
20d	4"
30d	4½"
40d	5"
50d	5½"
60d	6"

All nails used in fencing should be corrosion-resistant. Top-quality galvanized nails are preferred for most fence projects. Stainless steel or aluminum nails won't rust, but they're much more expensive than galvanized nails. Furthermore, aluminum nails are much weaker. Besides diameter and corrosion-resistance, nail length also affects holding power: Use nails that are three times as long as the thickness of the board they're expected to hold.

You may find nails identified by penny size, written as "d," which originally indicated the cost of 100 nails. The chart opposite shows the length of nails of different penny sizes. To compute the quantity you need,

decide on a likely nailing pattern for one section of fence. Count up the number of each size and type of nail required for that nailing pattern, multiply by the total number of fence sections, then add 10% to 15% for each type of nail.

Fence brackets are useful for attaching rails or siding between the posts; three common types are illustrated below. Brackets and other fasteners other than nails (bolts, screws, or staples) are estimated in a similar manner (number needed per section times number of sections plus 10% to 15%). All fasteners and metal hardware should be corrosion-resistant.

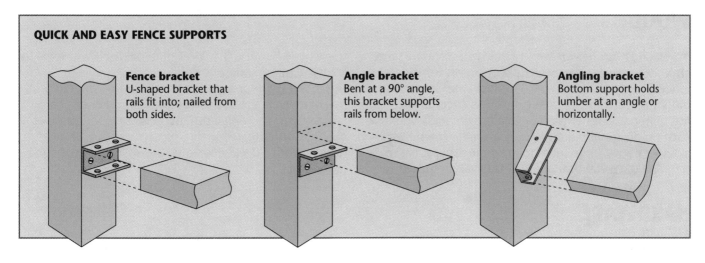

QUICK AND EASY FENCE SUPPORTS

Fence bracket
U-shaped bracket that rails fit into; nailed from both sides.

Angle bracket
Bent at a 90° angle, this bracket supports rails from below.

Angling bracket
Bottom support holds lumber at an angle or horizontally.

CONCRETE AND GRAVEL

Standard fence construction requires that posts be set in concrete (page 44), although lighter fences—such as some post-and-board or low picket fences—may have their posts set in earth-and-gravel fill. The amount of concrete or gravel needed will depend on the number and size of postholes, and how much of each hole will be filled by the post itself; estimating accurately isn't always easy.

Generally speaking, if you're setting 4-inch-diameter posts in concrete, you'll need 1/3 cubic foot of gravel in the bottom of each hole and 2/3 cubic foot of concrete. When setting posts in earth-and-gravel fill, you'll need

1/3 cubic foot of gravel for the bottom of the hole and 1 cubic foot to mix with the earth.

Unless you're fencing several acres, buying concrete ready-mixed in sacks (sand, gravel, cement—you add the water) is the most convenient in terms of ordering and then mixing on the job. A 90-pound sack of ready-mixed concrete makes about 2/3 cubic foot, so you can figure one bag for each post and hole.

You can buy gravel from garden centers, quarries, or building suppliers in almost any amount by the sack or by the truckload. Ask for it by the cubic foot or cubic yard (27 cubic feet equals 1 cubic yard).

FINISHES

For some ideas on finishing your fence, turn to page 79. To calculate the amount of paint or stain you'll need, calculate the total number of square feet of fence surface to be covered; then check the product's label for the manufacturer's estimate of coverage (number of square feet per gallon).

If your fence has a fairly solid, unbroken surface (panels, butted boards, louvers), simply multiply fence height

by overall length; add 10% to the figure to be sure you buy enough for the job. Double the amount if you plan to paint both sides.

If the fence has an open design (post and board, spaced lath, or pickets), estimate the square feet of board surface in each section; then multiply by the number of sections. Add 10% to the total. On all estimates, double the total if you're going to apply two coats.

GATE MATERIALS

Your gate is likely to get much more abuse than the rest of your fence, so make sure it's solidly constructed and attached with hardware that's sufficiently strong.

Generally, the same range of materials is available for gates as for fences: vinyl, metal, or wood. Vinyl gates can be purchased from a vinyl fencing company; see page 12 for a discussion of vinyl fencing. Metal gates include chain link or ornamental metal (wrought iron, aluminum, or tubular steel) types. All metal gates are prefabricated, either in stock designs available from gate manufacturers or custom made to your specifications.

Wood gates, on the other hand, can be designed and built by a do-it-yourselfer with moderate carpentry skills, as shown on pages 53 to 58. Or you can hire a carpenter or contractor to build the gate, either from your plans or theirs.

WOOD

In selecting lumber for wood gates, you have the same choices as for fences; see the section on lumber for fences, beginning on page 29. Most gates have diagonally braced frames made from 2x4s covered with siding material. Lighter frames—made from 2x2s or 2x3s with no diagonal bracing—can be used if the siding is exterior plywood, hardboard, or some other sheet material. The diagonal bracing is not usually required in these cases because the sheet material itself will serve to keep the frame square.

Lumber used for a gate frame should be straight and free of defects. Even slightly warped lumber can throw a whole gate out of alignment. Choose wood that has been pressure-treated with a preservative, or all-heart lumber from a decay-resistant species such as redwood or red cedar.

HARDWARE

Like other hardware for fences and gates *(page 32)*, latches and hinges should be rust- and corrosion-resistant.

LATCHES

Latches usually serve to keep a gate closed, but some types can also hold the gate open; two examples of latches that do this are shown at the top of page 36. The drawings on the opposite page illustrate the most commonly used gate hardware. More ornate styles of latches can be special ordered or custom made by a metal worker. If you're building a wooden gate, you can devise a wooden bolt like one illustrated opposite, or create your own design.

Whether you buy a latch or make your own, be sure it's sturdy enough for the gate and for the rough handling it will have to take. Use the longest screws or bolts possible when attaching the latch assembly.

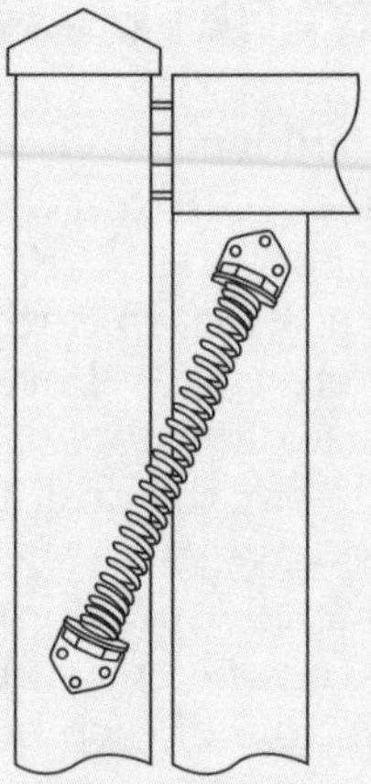

HINGES

Inadequate hinges are the principal cause of gate failure. It's better to use an overly strong hinge than to use one that's not strong enough. The nature of your gate siding will influence your choice of hinge. You may also want to buy hinges that match the latch, and sometimes this may call for a revision in the gate design.

If a fence is used to confine small children, self-closing hinges are a worthwhile investment; springs in the hinge mechanism automatically close the gate, which otherwise might be left ajar.

> ## ⏱ QUICK FIX
>
> **KEEPING A GATE SHUT**
> *If you find that your gate doesn't stay shut, install a gate spring. This heavy-duty spring will automatically pull the gate shut after you pass through. Attach the spring diagonally to the gate and gate post on the hinge side, as shown.*

Some of the more familiar hinges are illustrated on page 36. All of them do a good job, provided they are sized for the weight of the gate and attached with screws that are long enough. Many packaged hinges include fasteners that are too short for a heavy gate. Use screws that go as far into the wood as possible, without coming out the other side.

It's best to put three hinges on gates over 5 feet tall or more than 3 feet wide, unless you use heavy-duty hinges. A knowledgeable hardware dealer can assist you in choosing the right sized hinges for your gate.

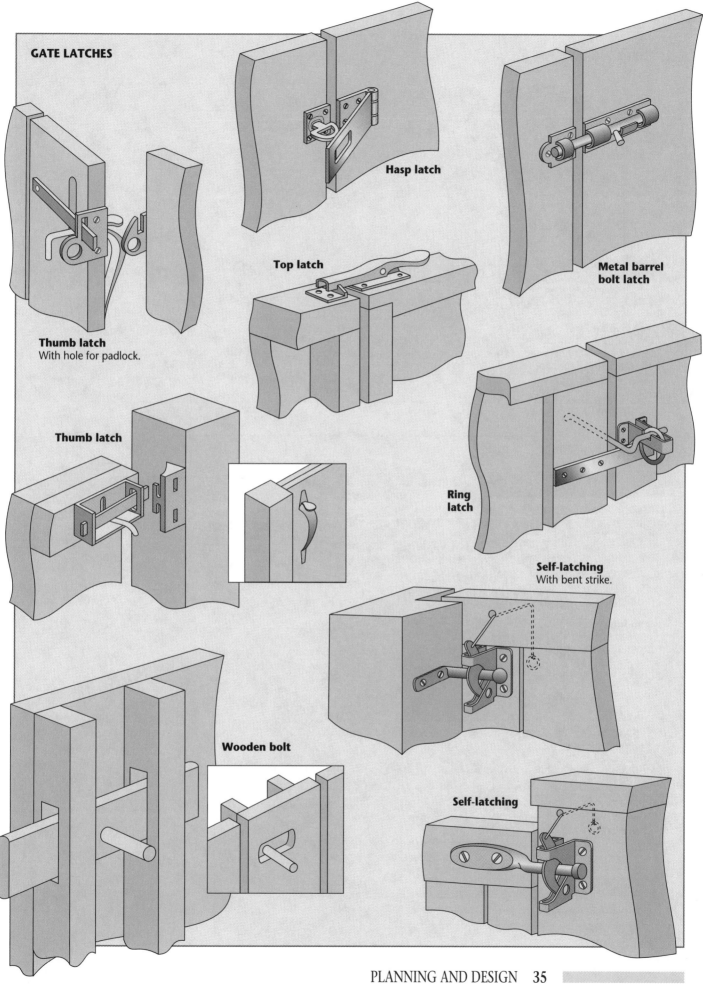

GATE LATCHES

Hasp latch

Metal barrel bolt latch

Top latch

Thumb latch
With hole for padlock.

Thumb latch

Ring latch

Self-latching
With bent strike.

Wooden bolt

Self-latching

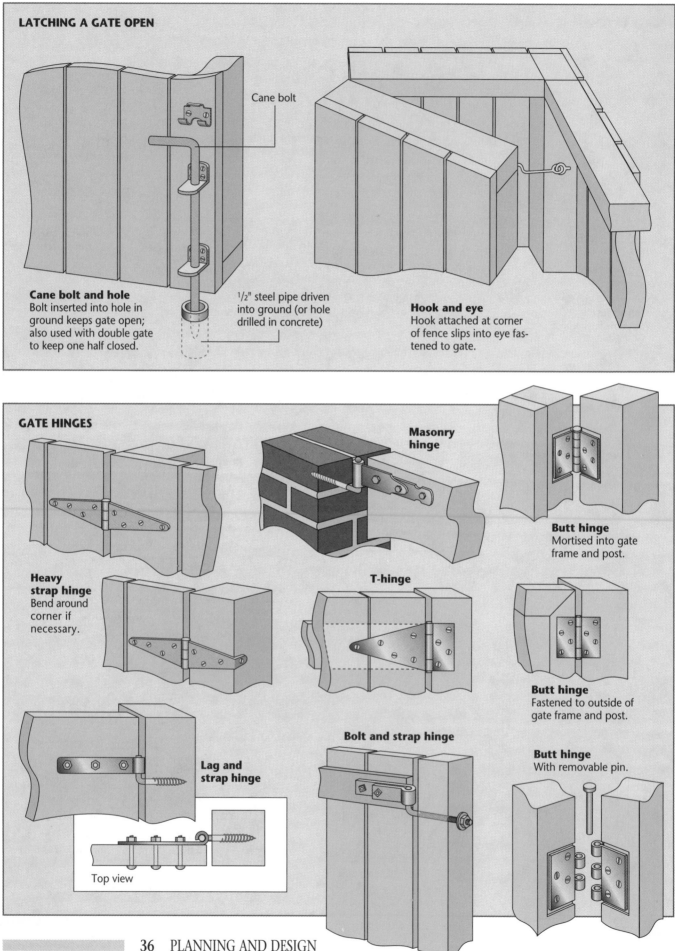

LATCHING A GATE OPEN

Cane bolt

Cane bolt and hole
Bolt inserted into hole in ground keeps gate open; also used with double gate to keep one half closed.

1/2" steel pipe driven into ground (or hole drilled in concrete)

Hook and eye
Hook attached at corner of fence slips into eye fastened to gate.

GATE HINGES

Masonry hinge

Butt hinge
Mortised into gate frame and post.

Heavy strap hinge
Bend around corner if necessary.

T-hinge

Butt hinge
Fastened to outside of gate frame and post.

Lag and strap hinge

Top view

Bolt and strap hinge

Butt hinge
With removable pin.

BUILDING FENCES AND GATES

Once your fence plans are complete, it's time to take them off the drafting board (or dining room table) and put them into action. After you've determined the quantities of materials you'll need and ordered them, the next step is to take your plans outside to begin construction.

Fence building can be divided into three stages: the relatively easy, preliminary stage of plotting the fence (locating and marking where posts will go); the somewhat more difficult stage of installing posts (digging holes, then setting and aligning posts); and the third, satisfying stage of adding the rails and siding.

You'll find the basic fence building methods outlined in this chapter; you can tailor the procedures to fit your specific situation. We'll also show you some specific constructions details for various types of fences, starting on page 59. You can customize a gate to go with any one of these fences by adapting the basic instructions for building a gate *(page 53)* to the fence style you've chosen.

You'll learn how to assemble fence posts and rails by cutting dadoes in the posts, as shown above. The rails can then be recessed in the dadoes.

BEFORE YOU BEGIN

To be sure you're not going to hit any pipelines or underground cables, have your utility companies mark the locations of cables and pipes on the ground, so you can dig safely.

Each of the three stages of fence building—plotting the fence, installing the posts, and attaching rails and siding—consists of a number of specific steps. The actual sequence of steps will vary according to the type of fence you build and other factors such as fence length and surrounding landscape conditions. Some builders, for instance, like to set all the posts and then attach rails and siding. This is often the easiest procedure for fences that have their posts set in concrete *(page 44)*.

Another method involves assembling the fence in sections, filling in the rails and siding as soon as two posts are in place. This is the method used for many prefabricated fences. If posts and rails are fitted together with interlocking joints, the rails may have to be attached before the posts are set.

Whatever method you choose, the tools you'll require are the same. You'll need a long tape measure (50 to 100 feet long is best) and a water level *(page 46)* for plotting the fence line, and a plumb bob to mark post locations accurately. You'll need a tool for digging postholes (an auger, posthole digger, or power auger, shown at right), perhaps a heavy digger bar for dealing with rocks, and a carpenter's level for aligning posts (2 feet long is recommended). You can buy a level specifically designed for this task; it bends around the post so you can read plumb in two directions without moving it.

You'll also need a carpenter's square to align rails with posts; a combination square; a hammer; a butt chisel; a circular saw or crosscut saw; an electric drill and the appropriate drill bits for boring pilot holes and mortising posts; and a shovel to fill postholes with concrete or earth and gravel. You may also need a small garden spade for removing excess earth from postholes, a saber saw for cutting pickets and C-clamps for holding the pickets while you cut them, and tools for mixing concrete *(page 43)*. Consider renting a pneumatic nailer to make nailing go faster.

Supplies that will come in handy include string to mark the fence line, chalk for marking post locations on the string, and a 3-foot-long piece of rod, pipe, or dowel to make a compass if you're planning curves.

If you're using pressure-treated lumber, brush any exposed surfaces made by cutting or drilling with a wood preservative containing at least 2% copper naphthenate. (Cut edges of decay-resistant lumber, such as redwood or cedar heartwood, don't need to be treated.) If you intend to paint your fence, you'll get the best results if you treat the lumber with a water repellent and apply the primer before you erect the fence.

Always follow safe working practices: Wear eye protection when using a striking tool such as a hammer; work gloves for handling rough lumber or sharp objects; and a dust mask or respirator when you may be inhaling dust or harmful products (such as when cutting pressure-treated lumber). When working with power tools, follow the manufacturer's operating instructions and wear hearing protection.

Remember that while fence building doesn't require any advanced technical skills, it's often physically difficult, so it's a good idea to have a helper.

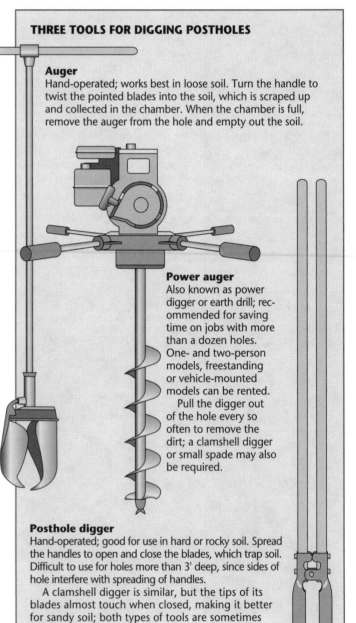

THREE TOOLS FOR DIGGING POSTHOLES

Auger
Hand-operated; works best in loose soil. Turn the handle to twist the pointed blades into the soil, which is scraped up and collected in the chamber. When the chamber is full, remove the auger from the hole and empty out the soil.

Power auger
Also known as power digger or earth drill; recommended for saving time on jobs with more than a dozen holes. One- and two-person models, freestanding or vehicle-mounted models can be rented.
Pull the digger out of the hole every so often to remove the dirt; a clamshell digger or small spade may also be required.

Posthole digger
Hand-operated; good for use in hard or rocky soil. Spread the handles to open and close the blades, which trap soil. Difficult to use for holes more than 3' deep, since sides of hole interfere with spreading of handles.
A clamshell digger is similar, but the tips of its blades almost touch when closed, making it better for sandy soil; both types of tools are sometimes called clamshell diggers.

PLOTTING THE FENCE

The first step in building your fence is to locate the exact course it will take and mark the line with stakes and string. If you're building the fence on or right next to a boundary or property line, you must be certain of the exact location of that line.

Of course, if the original survey stakes or markers still indicate the boundaries of your newly surveyed lot, you're fairly safe in using them for the fence line. Also, if the description of your property is exact enough in your deed, you might be able to measure the lines yourself. But if you're not absolutely certain of the line's position, have a surveyor or civil engineer lay out the corner stakes of your property. Though such a survey will cost you a fee, it will cost much less than moving the fence later.

If you're replacing an existing boundary or division fence, don't assume that the original one was built exactly on the line. Check your survey and that of your neighbors to avoid any possible misunderstanding.

If, after checking all sources of information, you still have doubts about the location of the boundaries, you may want to set the posts at least 6 inches inside the line just to be safe. For a discussion of the legal aspects of boundary fencing, see page 21.

If you're not building a boundary fence—if your fence or screen will lie within your property—simply measure the desired length of the fence line and mark the location of end and corner posts. Below and on the next two pages, we'll show you how to mark right angles and curves and how to plot hillside fences.

If you've planned a fence for a hillside with a very steep or irregular slope, it's best to have a professional lay out and build the fence. But if the slope is fairly gradual and uniform (no large humps or depressions along the fence line), you can plot it yourself, using one of the methods described below.

To establish the fence line, you'll need a 50- to 100-foot tape measure; a ball of mason's twine or any non-stretchable, tightly twisted nylon string, such as braided fishing line; some stakes (available precut at lumberyards); a hammer (to drive the stakes); some large common nails; a few scraps of paper; and a piece of colored chalk. To transfer post locations from the twine to the ground, you'll need a plumb bob.

Plotting a straight fence

TOOLKIT
• Claw hammer
• Tape measure
• Plumb bob (optional)

1 Setting up the fence line
Use a hammer to drive a stake at each end or corner post location. Then run mason's twine or string between two stakes, drawing it tight and tying it firmly to each stake. Ideally, the twine should be as close to the ground as possible, but if bushes or other obstructions are in the way, use tall stakes so the twine can be attached high enough to clear them.

If the fence line is very long, you may have to prop up the twine with intermediate stakes every 100' or so to keep it from sagging. Make sure the additional stakes are aligned with the first two.

2 ▶ Marking the post locations
Locate the intermediate posts by measuring along the twine and marking their centers on the twine with chalk. If the twine is close to the ground, simply depress it and push a nail through a piece of paper into the ground to mark the post's location along the fence line *(near right)*.

If the twine is more than a few inches off the ground, use a plumb bob to locate the center of the post and set the nail marker in the ground *(far right)*.

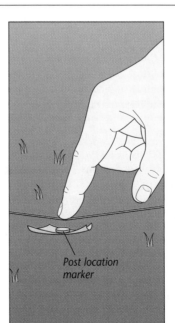

Post location marker

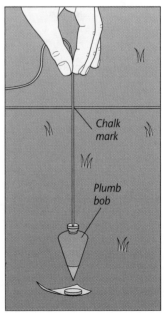

Chalk mark

Plumb bob

Using the 3-4-5 method

To plot a 90° angle, set up the first fence line (point A to point B), as described on page 39. Stretch another length of twine roughly perpendicular to the first. On the first fence line (AB), measure and chalk-mark the twine 4' from the corner stake (B), then mark the second fence line (BC) 3' from the corner stake.

Adjust the second fence line until the diagonal measurement between the two marks equals 5', as shown below. Because twine stretches when pulled, check the location of the 3' mark before measuring the diagonal each time you adjust the second fence line.

When you've established a 90° angle, drive a stake and tie the twine to it.

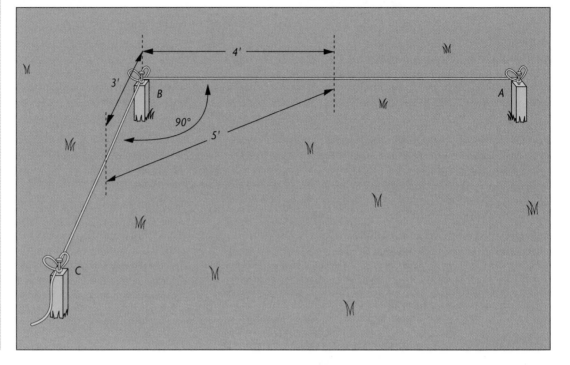

Plotting a curve

TOOLKIT
- Tape measure
- Claw hammer for driving stakes
- Chalk line for marking twine

Using a compass

You don't have to be a mathematician to plot a symmetrical curve in your fence line, but you will need to make a very large compass for scribing your arc in the dirt.

Start by stretching twine between the end stakes of the intended curve. Then, measure to find the midpoint between the two end stakes and drive a stake at this location. From this center stake, run a second line at 90° to the first, as explained above, roughly equal in length to the first line.

Drive a 3' long rod, pipe, or dowel as a pivot point along the second line. The farther away from the fence line you drive the pivot post, the shallower the arc will be *(red dotted line)*; you may have to try several positions before you get the desired arc.

Measure a length of cord to reach from the pivot post to one of the end stakes, then attach one end of the cord to the pivot post and the other end to a pointed stick. Keeping the line taut, scribe an arc in the ground from one end stake to the other, as shown at right. To locate the intermediate posts, bend a flexible tape measure on edge around the arc and mark the desired post spacing.

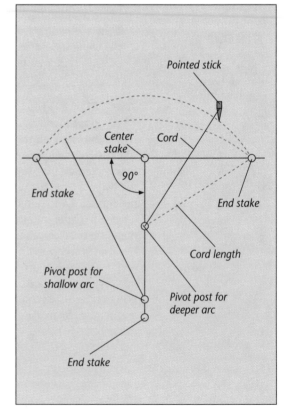

Plotting contour hillside fencing

TOOLKIT
- Claw hammer for driving stakes
- Tape measure
- Plumb bob

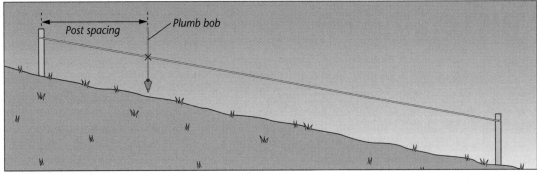

Following the slope

Drive end stakes and stretch twine between them; the twine should be high enough to clear the ground between the stakes. For rolling or uneven terrain, you may have to drive intermediate stakes to keep the twine at a uniform height.

Measure and chalk-mark the intermediate post locations on the string. Then use a plumb bob to transfer the marks to the ground beneath *(above)*. Drive nails through pieces of paper to mark the ground, as described on page 39.

Plotting stepped hillside fencing

TOOLKIT
- Claw hammer to drive stakes
- Tape measure
- Water level

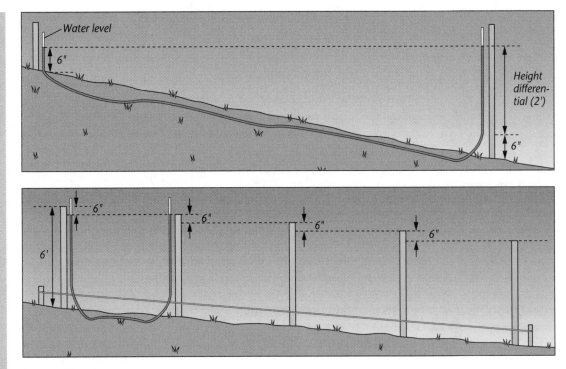

Descending in steps

Drive end stakes, using a tall stake at the downhill end so its top end is at about the same elevation as the top of the uphill end stake. Mark a point 6" from the ground on the uphill stake and hold one end of a water level alongside the stake so that the water levels off at the mark. Hold the other end against the downhill stake until the water finds its level; mark that point.

Measure down from this point to the ground, then subtract 6" to get the height differential of the slope *(above, top)*; 2' in this example. Divide the height differential by the number of fence sections to find the amount of drop per section. Here, 2' divided by four gives a 6" drop per section. Mark the post locations as for contour fencing *(step above)*.

When you're ready to install the posts, remove the stakes and twine, dig the postholes *(page 42)*, and relocate the stakes and twine to one side of their original position (for 4x4 posts, move the stakes 2").

Set the post at the uphill end of the fence to the desired height (6'); then measure the amount of drop (6") from the top of the post and mark it on the side facing the location of the next post. Set the next post loosely in the hole. Hold one end of a water level at the mark on the first post and the other end against the second post. Adjust the height of the second post until it's level *(above, bottom)*. Continue this process with the successive posts until they're all set.

INSTALLING POSTS

Installing posts is the most important part of fence building. If posts are not set firmly in the ground, they'll be the weak part of an otherwise solidly built fence. They must be plumb (aligned vertically) in their holes and located exactly in line or you'll encounter difficulties when adding rails and siding materials.

The process can be divided into three steps: digging the postholes, setting the posts, and aligning the posts. The size of the holes depends on the height and weight of the fence, the stresses it must withstand, and the soil conditions on your lot.

Setting and aligning posts is best done by two people —one to hold and align the post while the other fills the hole with concrete or earth and gravel. The most critical step in post installation is aligning the posts so that they're exactly vertical and in a straight line. Many fence designs call for posts set at precisely the same height so that their tops are level with each other. Examples include fences with rails attached to the top of the posts, and fences with rails recessed into posts by means of a notch or dado.

Fence posts are generally set in concrete, but some may be set in earth-and-gravel fill. If the soil is stable (not subject to sliding, cracking, or frost heaving), earth-and-gravel fill is adequate for lightweight fences—such as lath, picket, and some post-and-board—or for fences 4 feet or less in height. In some cases, especially if your fence is not very long, you can use commercial post holders, which allow you to set posts without digging, and without concrete or earth and gravel.

To install fence posts you'll need a digging tool *(page 38)*; perhaps a digger/tamper bar (a heavy metal bar with one sharp end and one flat end) to break up or loosen rocks and very hard soil; tools for mixing concrete *(opposite)*; a shovel, hammer, tape measure, and 2-foot carpenter's level; and a water level for adjusting post height. To make your own water level, see page 46.

In the following pages, we'll tell you how to set posts in earth and gravel or in concrete, as well as various ways to align posts and adjust their height. If the posts are to be cut (dadoed or mortised) to accept rails *(page 50)*, you can either cut the posts before setting them, which means you'll have to set all the posts to exactly the same height, or you can set the posts first and then cut them. If you choose the second option, making the cuts is trickier and you'll have to cut each post individually.

PLAY IT SAFE

USING A POWER AUGER
Usually gas-powered, power augers are powerful tools that should be used with caution. Be careful not to touch the hot motor, and dig only about one foot at a time, keeping a keen lookout for rocks and roots. It the auger hits something hard and stops, you may be thrown off balance. Stop working when you're fatigued—using a power auger requires full concentration.

Digging postholes

TOOLKIT
- Posthole digger, hand auger, or power auger
- Digger/tamper bar (optional)
- Tape measure

Determining the depth and diameter of postholes
The tools you use to dig postholes will depend on the number of postholes and the type of soil you have. If the ground is very hard to work, or you've planned quite a few postholes, you may want to rent a power digging tool or hire someone to do the digging. Turn to page 38 for guidelines on using the appropriate tools for digging postholes.

For residential fencing between 3' and 6' tall, set posts a minimum of 2' deep. Posts are commonly available in 6', 7', and 8' lengths for 4', 5', and 6' fences, respectively. Since end posts and gate posts need more support, use posts 1' longer, and set them 1' deeper than line posts. If your fence is over 6' tall, subject to unusual stresses (high winds, unstable soil, or heavy siding materials) or frost heaving

(page 44), or if it's used to contain large animals, you may need to set the posts deeper than 2'. A good rule to follow in these situations is to sink posts at least one third of their total length into the ground and set them in concrete. Local fence contractors may be willing to advise you on soil conditions that affect fence building in your area and offer suggestions for setting posts.

Make the hole diameter 2$\frac{1}{2}$ to 3 times the post's width or diameter (for round posts); 10" to 12" for 4" thick posts. The bottom of the posthole should be slightly wider than the top to provide a solid base. To allow water to drain past the bottom of the post, dig the hole 4" to 6" deeper than the post will be set and fill the bottom with rocks and gravel.

Setting a post: earth and gravel

TOOLKIT
- Tape measure
- Shovel
- Digger/tamper bar (optional)
- Carpenter's level
- Circular saw or crosscut saw (optional)
- Claw hammer (optional)

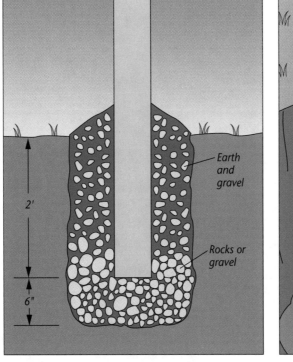

Earth and gravel

Rocks or gravel

2'

6"

Post

1x4 support

Securing the post
Place 4" to 6" of rocks or gravel in the hole, to encourage proper drainage. Or, place a large rock in the hole and surround it with rocks or gravel. Tamp the gravel using a 2x4 or the flat end of a digger/tamper bar. Set the post in the hole and shovel in earth and gravel until the hole is filled *(above, left)*. After adding every 2" or 3" of fill, align the post and plumb it with a level, and tamp the earth and gravel firmly.

If the hole is wide, jam big rocks around the post near the surface to minimize lateral movement. In light, sandy soil—which offers poor stability—cut short lengths of 1x4 heartwood cedar or redwood, or pressure-treated wood, and nail them across the posts near ground level *(above, right)*.

Finally, slope the top of the fill so that water will run away from the post.

ASK A PRO

HOW DO I MIX MY OWN CONCRETE?

For most fence projects, using dry, premixed concrete (cement, sand, and gravel, all in one bag) is easiest. But you can mix your own concrete, using a mix of two parts (by volume) cement, three parts sand, and five parts gravel. When you add the water, keep the mix rather stiff (dry) to avoid having dirt from the hole infiltrate the concrete, and to keep the post in alignment.

Concrete can be mixed by hand or by machine; for setting fence posts, you'll only need small amounts at a time (about 2/3 cubic foot per post), so it's best to mix it by hand. You can use a high-sided contractor's wheelbarrow to mix up to 2 cubic feet at a time or use a large piece of plywood or a mortar box (from a masonry supply store, or use a large plastic tub). Using a wheelbarrow is a good idea because you can transport the mixed concrete more easily.

Work with small amounts at a time; 2/3 cubic foot of dry ingredients makes 2/3 cubic foot of concrete. You can measure

the ingredients with a shovel—just make sure your scoopfuls are uniform. Use a container whose volume you know to measure the approximate volume of a shovelful. Keep a drum or bucket of clean water nearby that you can bail from; it's much more convenient than turning a tap on and off.

Place the sand on the mixing surface. Add the cement and mix thoroughly. Then add the gravel and mix again. Mound up the mixture and hollow out the center. Add a little bit of water to the hollow. Work around the sides of the hollow, pulling the dry ingredients into the water, always enlarging the size of the hollow.

Mix until the concrete is all the same color and all the dry ingredients are damp. Add more water, if necessary, a little at a time. The concrete should be stiff and you should be able to pack it into a ball with your hand. If it's too wet, add some sand and cement mixed together; use two parts cement to three parts sand.

Setting a post: concrete

TOOLKIT
- Shovel
- Carpenter's level
- Mason's trowel

Casting the concrete

Place a large stone in the posthole and shovel in 4" to 6" of rocks or gravel. Then place the post in the hole and add 4" more of rocks or gravel. This will keep the concrete from getting under the post and trapping water, which will speed decay.

Once your post is in the hole and ready to be set, mix the concrete and shovel it in evenly around the post. As you fill, tamp the concrete with a broomstick or the capped end of a steel pipe to work out any air pockets in the mix. Using a carpenter's level, check and adjust the post for alignment.

Continue filling until the concrete extends 1" or 2" above ground level and slope it away from the post to divert water (right); use a mason's trowel to slope it. You can place washed rocks around the perimeter of the hole to support the concrete above the hole.

Posts freshly set in concrete can be forced into alignment and plumb for about 20 minutes; they should then be left to sit for two days before rails and siding are nailed on.

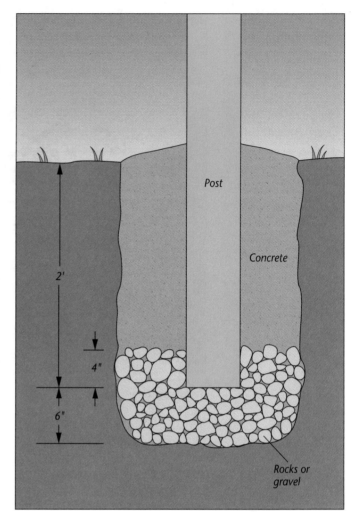

Post

Concrete

2'

4"

6"

Rocks or gravel

ASK A PRO

WHAT IF I LIVE IN A COLD CLIMATE?

Frozen ground in winter causes frost heaving (the shifting of ground caused by alternate freezing and thawing of the soil). To minimize damage from heaving, dig postholes down to 1 foot below the normal frost line and shovel in several inches of gravel. Drive nails partway into the sides of the post near its bottom end and place this end in the gravel. Shovel concrete around the nail area, then fill the hole with concrete (right). Make sure the post remains plumb as you work.

Another option is to dig the base of the hole below the frost line wider than the shaft of the hole, creating a bell shape at the bottom. Shovel gravel into the hole to a depth of about 4 to 6 inches, and set the end of the post in it, then fill the hole with concrete. The wider base will help keep the post stable.

There are also additives available that affect the performance of the concrete—to make it set faster, or to make it impervious to water, for example—so you may be able to adjust your mix for your particular needs.

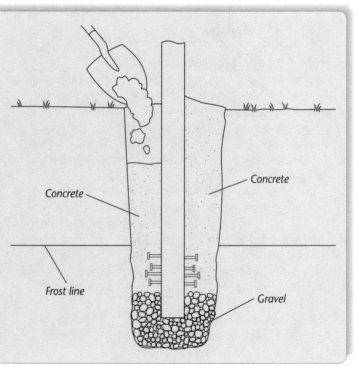

Concrete

Concrete

Frost line

Gravel

TOOLKIT
- Carpenter's level
- Tape measure
- Circular saw or crosscut saw
- Claw hammer
- Shovel

Using spacer blocks and string

For relatively short sections of fence (less than 100'), you can use a carpenter's level along with spacers and string to align posts. Start by positioning two corner or end posts so their faces are parallel, then plumb them with a level and set them permanently *(page 42)*.

Next, cut 2" long spacer blocks from 1x2 lumber and tack them to the end posts about 2' above ground level. Stretch twine between the two end posts, attaching it around the spacer blocks. The blocks will keep the intermediate posts from touching the string and throwing it out of alignment.

Set and align the intermediate posts at a distance away from the string that is exactly equal to the thickness of the spacer block; hold a spare spacer block against each post to measure this distance. Plumb each post on two adjacent faces as you set it *(below)*.

Carefully fill the holes, checking that each post remains vertical as you work. Once all the posts are set, make a final check by eye to be sure the posts have remained in alignment. Keep in mind that posts set in concrete can be adjusted for up to 20 minutes after the concrete is cast; after that they should not be moved.

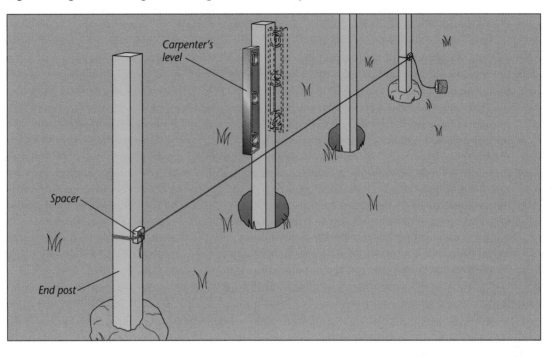

Carpenter's level

Spacer

End post

ASK A PRO

HOW DO I USE A LEVEL TO CHECK POSTS FOR PLUMB?
Hold one edge of the level flush against one side of the post, then adjust the position of the post until the bubble in the horizontal vial is centered between the lines. This tells you that the post is plumb in one direction. Repeat the process with the level against an adjacent side of the post to plumb it in the other direction. The post will then be vertical.

TOOLKIT
- Tape measure
- Claw hammer for driving stakes
- Carpenter's level

Aligning and setting posts successively

For very long sections of fence, such as country fencing, the method described above may be impractical because the string stretched between the end posts will sag. One way to solve this problem is to build the fence in sections, using the corner post method for about every 100'.

Or you can align and set posts successively—one after the other—until you reach the end of the fence line. This method should be used when building a mortised post-and-rail fence *(page 60)*. Move the stakes you used for plotting the fence *(page 39)* 2" to one side of the post centers and reconnect the twine. Line up the posts, using the twine as a guide. Use a level to plumb each post. Be careful not to move the twine out of alignment when setting the posts.

Setting a post alone

TOOLKIT
- Circular saw or crosscut saw
- Claw hammer
- Shovel
- Carpenter's level

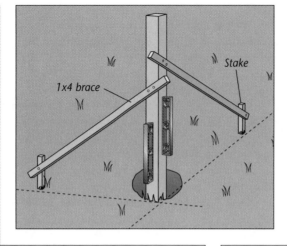

1x4 brace

Stake

Using braces

To install posts without a helper, set up braces to hold the posts as you align and set them in concrete or earth-and-gravel fill. Make the braces from 6' lengths of 1x4s fastened to stakes. Drive the stakes into the ground and attach the braces with one nail so they can be pivoted and then fastened to two adjacent sides of the post *(left)*.

As explained below, this method works with either concrete or earth-and-gravel fill. If you're using concrete, make enough braces to hold four posts (eight braces in all) so you can set additional posts while the concrete hardens around the first post.

Setting posts in earth-and-gravel fill

Place a base stone and 6" of rocks or gravel in the bottom of the hole. Position the post in the hole and hold it vertical while you shovel in enough earth and gravel to support the post and still leave it adjustable. Use a level on adjacent post faces to align the post vertically *(page 45)*.

Being careful not to move the post out of alignment, tack the braces to the post; make sure they'll be easy to remove later. Fill the remainder of the hole with earth and gravel *(page 43)*. As you work, check the alignment of the post frequently with your level and adjust the braces if necessary. When the post is firmly set, carefully remove the braces and use them on the next post.

Setting posts in concrete

Place a base stone and 6" of gravel into the hole, insert the post, and, holding the post vertical, pivot the braces and attach them to the post. Just tack the nails in so they can be removed easily later.

Fill the hole with concrete *(page 44)*. Check the post for plumb with a carpenter's level. If necessary, remove the braces and align the post, then reattach the braces, being careful not to move the post out of alignment. Let the concrete set for at least an hour before removing the braces.

Meanwhile, use the three additional sets of braces to install successive posts. By the time the fourth post is set, the braces on the first post can be removed and used on the fifth.

ASK A PRO

HOW DOES A WATER LEVEL WORK?

A water level is essentially a length of plastic tubing filled with water. If you hold up both ends of the tube, the water will be at the same height at each end because a body of water always seeks its own level. You can use a water level to level across distances, such as between the end posts of a fence.

You can buy a commercial water level or make your own using clear plastic tubing or clear hose at least $1/4$ inch in diameter; add food coloring to the water to make reading easier. To fill the tubing, hold one end in a bucket of water. Suck on the other end while holding it lower than the bucket, until the water enters the tube. This creates a siphon; the water will flow by itself to fill the tube. To make sure there are no air bubbles, which will throw off the level, let a little water flow out the loose end. When you hold up both ends, the water levels should be even. If they're not, empty the tube and fill it again.

To use a water level, you and a helper must hold both ends up. At one end, line up the water's height with a reference point—the pencil mark on a post, for example. To transfer

that point to the next post, place the other end against the post and mark the height of the water; the two marks will be level. To store the level, plug the ends with rubber stoppers or cork plugs, or empty the tube and refill it the next time.

Clear plastic tubing filled with water

Fence post

Adjusting post height

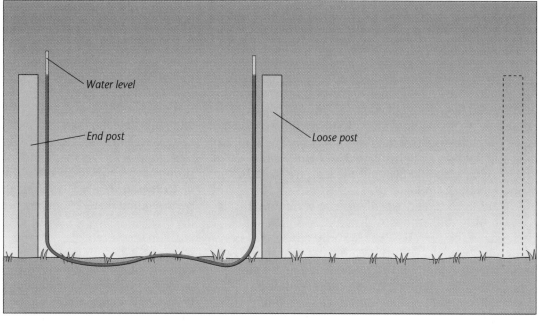

Using a water level

Set one end post to the desired height and place the next post loosely in its hole. Hold up both ends of a water level and move them together to line up the level of the water at one end of the tube with the top of the post. Hold the other end against the loose post and adjust the post up or down until its top is level with the water *(above)*. Then set the loose post firmly in place.

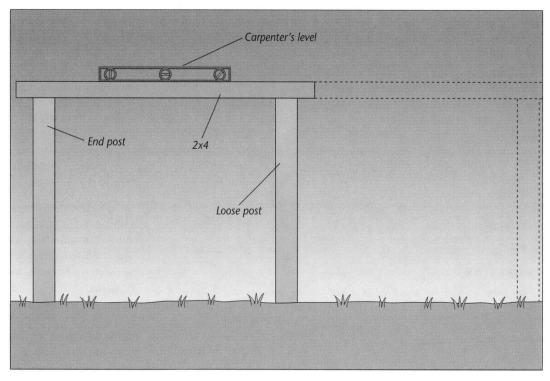

Using a carpenter's level

You can also adjust post height using a carpenter's level. Set the end post to the desired height and place the next post loosely in its hole. Lay a straight 2x4 across the tops of the two posts *(above)*. (To pick a straight 2x4, sight down the end.) Center a carpenter's level on top of the 2x4 and hold it in position. Check for level while a helper adjusts and sets the loose post. Repeat the procedure for the subsequent posts.

ADDING RAILS AND SIDING

Once the fence posts are set and aligned, the hardest part is over. The next step is to install the rails and siding (boards, pickets, panels, or other material) on the posts. If the rails are not attached firmly and squarely to the posts, all of your painstaking work in aligning the posts will be wasted. Remember that posts set in concrete should be left for at least two days before you attach rails and siding.

Fastening rails: Fence builders use several methods for fastening rails to posts, depending on the fence design and the materials used. Many fences use 4x4 posts and 2x4 rails, with the siding attached to the rails. With others, notably post-and-board or post-and-rail types, the rails and siding are one and the same.

No matter what type of fence you'll be building, there are a limited number of ways to attach rails to posts, as shown below and on the following pages. You can butt the rails between the posts; recess the rails into the posts by means of a dado or a notch; lap the rails over the sides or tops of the posts (for a stronger fence, be sure to make the rails long enough to span three posts); or pass the rails through a mortise in the post. Dadoes, notches, and mortises should be cut before the posts are set. For contour hillside fencing *(page 24)*, there are only two practical methods of joinery—lapping rails over the sides of posts or mortising rails into them.

Because the joints between rails and posts will trap moisture, your first step should be to apply a finish or wood preservative as protection against decay to all surfaces where the rails and posts come into contact. This is recommended even if the wood used for rails is pressure-treated lumber or is from a decay-resistant species *(page 29)*. For pressure-treated lumber, copper naphthenate is the recommended chemical; you can find it at hardware stores and home centers. However, this chemical will tint your wood green, so try to keep it off surfaces that will be visible. For any product you choose, check the label to see if it will color the wood, and if it can be painted or stained over. Also read and follow the safety precautions that are printed on the label.

Attaching siding: How you attach siding will depend on the siding material and on your fence design. Attaching boards, slats, pickets, or grapestakes is simple but tedious—for example, 100 feet of grapestake fencing require 1,200 nails on the siding alone. If you're attaching panels (plywood, hardboard, or other material) the work will go more quickly, but you'll probably need a helper to lift the panels into position and hold them steady while you do the nailing. Specific techniques for attaching siding on different styles of fences are discussed later in this chapter, beginning on page 59.

Installing kickboards: On wood fences, the siding usually ends 6 to 8 inches above the ground to keep it from rotting at ground level. If you want to close this gap, a kickboard can be installed at the bottom of the fence before the siding is attached. Kickboards are typically 1-by lumber, either pressure-treated or decay-resistant wood. They're centered between the posts under the bottom rail, or attached to the sides of the posts and bottom rail. In some cases, such as to discourage animals from digging under the fence, you may want the kickboard to extend 4 to 6 inches into the ground.

Kickboards also prevent soil movement under the fence—important if you or your neighbors decide to build a raised planter bed next to the fence or otherwise change the soil level in your yards.

Butting rails between posts

TOOLKIT
• Claw hammer
• Electric drill (optional)
• Carpenter's square

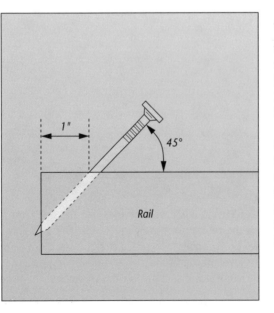

1"

45°

Rail

1 Starting the nails
Butting the rails against the posts is common for fences with 4x4 posts and 2x4 rails to which wood siding is attached. The rails are cut to fit snugly between the posts, then toenailed in place with 3" galvanized nails. To avoid splitting the rail ends, blunt the nail tips with a hammer before nailing.

To start the nails, lay the rail on the ground and drive the nails in until their tips barely protrude from the end of the rail. Use two nails at each end of the rail, slanting them at a 45° angle about 1" from the end of the rail *(left)*. If the ends of the rails still split easily when nailed, drill pilot holes for the nails, using an electric drill fitted with a bit two-thirds the diameter of the nail shank.

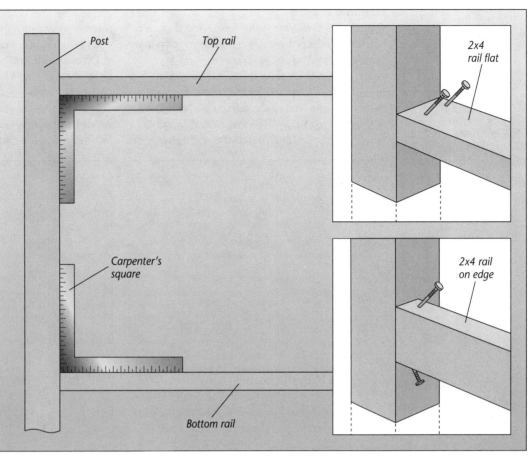

Post — Top rail — 2x4 rail flat

Carpenter's square

2x4 rail on edge

Bottom rail

2 Attaching the rails

With a helper holding the rail level at the other end, position the rail between the posts so the rail edges are flush with the post's front and back faces *(inset, top)*; use a carpenter's square to make sure each rail is perpendicular to the posts *(above)*. Then drive the nails into the post.

For fences with 2x4 rails and heavy siding—such as 1" boards or 3/4" plywood panels—place the bottom rail on edge *(inset, bottom)*. This will prevent the fence from sagging under its own weight. In this case, drive the nails through the top and bottom edges of the rail.

ASK A PRO

HOW DO I ATTACH THE RAILS FOR A CURVED FENCE?

If you've bent the rails to the shape of the curve (page 25), you simply need to hold the rail in place, making sure it's level, and nail it to the outside of the post. But if you're using straight lumber, you'll need to adapt one of the methods discussed above to form an angle. For example, you can lap the rails across the front of the posts and nail them in place; miter the ends of the rails for a seamless fit (right, top). Or you can cut the rails to fit between the posts. Again, you'll need to cut the rail ends on an angle so they butt against the post (right, bottom).

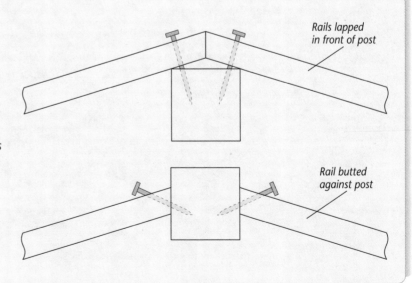

Rails lapped in front of post

Rail butted against post

Planning the job

You can recess rails into posts by cutting dadoes or notches into the posts, making a stronger joint than simply butting the pieces together.

You'll find that it's easier to cut dadoes and notches before the posts are set. To keep the cuts in alignment from one post to the next, you'll have to set all the posts to exactly the same height *(page 47)*. When you mark cutting lines on the posts, always measure down from the top of the post for both top and bottom rail positions.

On all but the end or corner posts, cut the dadoes or notches directly opposite each other on both sides of the post. In 4x4 posts, cut dadoes or notches no deeper than $1/2$"; otherwise the posts will be weakened. To attach the rails to the posts, slide the rails into the notches or dadoes and toenail them in place.

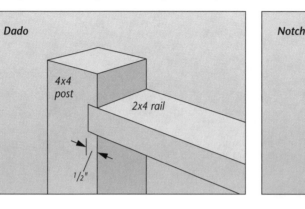

Making a dado or notch

TOOLKIT
- C-clamps
- Combination square or carpenter's square
- Circular saw
- Handsaw for notches
- Butt chisel
- Mallet

1 ▸ **Marking the posts**

To make sure the cuts line up, mark several posts at once, setting them on a work surface with their ends aligned and clamping a straightedge across the top of the pieces. Mark the depth of the cut on the outside pieces, then outline the width of the cuts using a pencil and combination square *(right)* or carpenter's square.

For a notch, mark the angle of the cut when outlining the depth of cut.

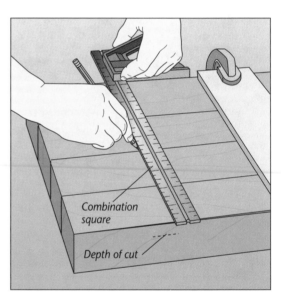

Combination square

Depth of cut

◂2 **Making the cuts**

If you're using a circular saw, measure from the saw blade to each side of the base plate and mark these two points on the posts on each side of your marked lines. Reposition the straightedge guide along one of the marks and make the cut, holding the base plate tight against the guide. Relocate the guide and cut the other side *(left)*; then, make several cuts between the first two. If you're sawing a notch, make the angled cuts in both the posts and rails with a handsaw.

To remove the waste between the saw kerfs, use a chisel, holding it bevel side down and tapping it lightly with a mallet *(inset)*.

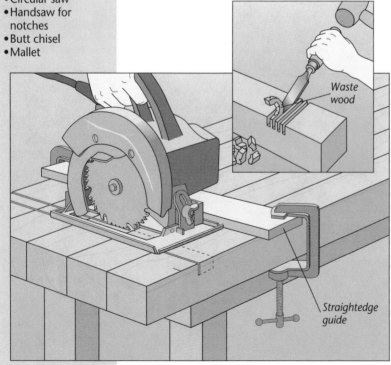

Waste wood

Straightedge guide

Lapping rails over posts

TOOLKIT
- Tape measure
- Combination square
- Circular saw or handsaw
- Claw hammer
- Backsaw and miter box (optional)

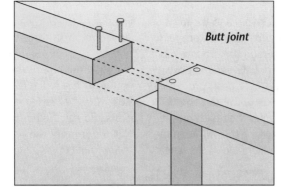

Butt joint

Mitered joint

Installing the rails

Lapping the rails across the posts is the easiest way to connect them.

On some types of fences, such as picket or board, the top rail is lapped across the tops of the posts *(above, left)*. In these cases, the ends of rails that meet at a corner post *(above, right)*, are cut with a backsaw and a miter box. Fasten the rails to the posts with galvanized nails three times as long as the rail thickness.

For post-and-board fences, the boards are lapped across the sides of the posts. Cut the rails long enough to span three posts so that the ends of the rails meet in the center of the post; stagger the joints on the top, middle (if any), and bottom rails.

Mortising a post

TOOLKIT
- Tape measure
- Combination square
- Electric drill
- Mallet
- Butt chisel

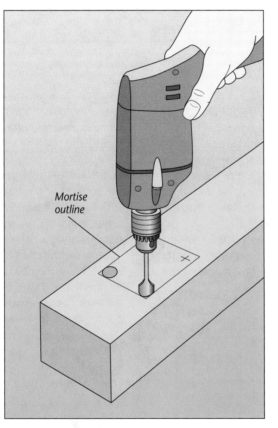

Mortise outline

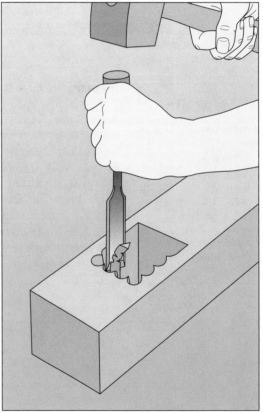

Cutting mortises

On many post-and-rail fences, the rails pass through mortises—rectangular holes—cut through the posts. You may be able to find posts with precut mortises, or you can make your own.

As with dadoes and notches, cutting mortises before setting the posts is easiest, but you'll have to be sure to set the posts to exactly the same height. To outline a mortise, lay the post across two sawhorses.

Measuring from the top of the post, use a combination square and a pencil to mark the cut lines. To cut the mortise, drill a series of overlapping holes within the outline through the post, using an electric drill fitted with a 1" spade bit; drill the corner holes first *(above, left)*. If necessary, turn the post over and drill from the other side, then use a mallet and butt chisel to remove the rest *(above, right)*.

Installing kickboards

TOOLKIT
• Shovel (optional)
• Circular saw
• Carpenter's level
• Claw hammer

Attaching the boards

You can either attach the kickboards to the front of the posts, or center them under the bottom rails. Unless the kickboards will rest on the ground, dig a narrow trench, 4" to 6" deep, between the posts.

Attaching the kickboards to the posts provides a ledge on which to set the siding. Cut the boards to span two fence sections. Center their ends on the posts and level them *(below, left)*; this will keep the pieces of siding at an even height along the fence line. Fasten the kickboards to the posts and rails with galvanized nails three times the boards' thickness; butt the ends of adjoining boards together.

Center the boards under the bottom rails when you want the fence to look the same on both sides. Cut 1x1 strips to fit snugly between the posts and nail them on each side of the kickboard. Nail the strips to the bottom rails from underneath *(below, right)*.

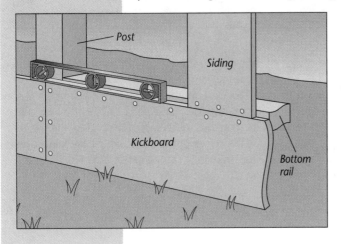

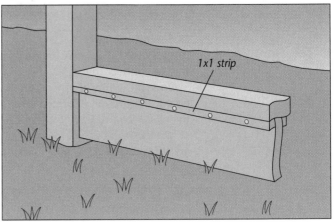

Attaching siding

TOOLKIT
• Tape measure
• Circular saw
• Carpenter's level
• Claw hammer
• Electric drill (optional)
• Pneumatic nailer (optional)

Aligning the boards

To keep siding at an even height along the fence line, make sure all the pieces are cut to the same length. If you've installed kickboards on the sides of the posts as shown above, you can set the siding pieces on top of them. Otherwise, stretch and level a string from post to post at the height above the ground where you want the bottom of the siding.

Position the first board and check it for plumb with a carpenter's level. If the boards fit tightly together, simply butt each board against the preceding one. If the boards are spaced a few inches apart, rip a spacer to the appropriate width, and use it to keep the boards aligned.

Periodically check the vertical alignment of the boards with a carpenter's level and be sure to align the bottoms of the boards with the string *(below, left)*. Fasten the boards with galvanized nails three times as long as the thickness of the siding. The number of nails depends on the width of the boards; see the chart below. To avoid splitting the wood, blunt the nail tips with a hammer before driving them. If you're nailing less than 1" from the ends of the boards or pickets and splitting occurs, drill pilot holes for the nails with a bit slightly smaller than the shanks' diameter.

Consider renting a pneumatic nailer to attach siding; follow the operating instructions that come with the tool.

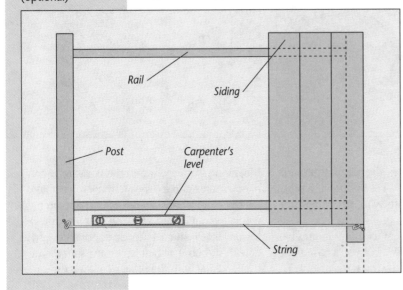

NUMBER OF NAILS	
Lumber width (nominal)	Nails required across width
2"	1
3" 4" 6"	2
8"	3

BUILDING A GATE

The standard sequence for gate construction is to set and align gateposts, build the frame, add siding, hang the gate, and, finally, install the latch.

For the most part, these procedures are quite simple, but they do require precise workmanship. A few miscalculations in gatepost alignment, or in measuring, cutting, and assembling gate components, will result in a gate that won't open and close smoothly. The gate must be built solidly and attached firmly to the post with heavy-duty hinges, or it will likely start to sag and bind soon after installation.

If you feel the required carpentry is beyond your ability, especially if your design calls for detailed joinery work, you might prefer to have this part of your fence erected by a contractor or a carpenter with gate-building experience.

GATEPOSTS

Gateposts must be set deeper than fence posts because of the added stress placed on them. They must also be lined up perfectly and plumbed vertically so that their inside faces are exactly parallel. The posts must be set firmly in concrete or they'll soon lean, hampering the gate's smooth operation.

Setting gateposts

TOOLKIT
• Carpenter's level
• Tape measure
• Water level or line level (optional)

Aligning the posts
Set the posts as you would a fence post *(page 42)* so at least one third of their total length is below ground; for a 6' tall gate, use 9' posts and sink them 3' deep.

Plumb the posts vertically using a carpenter's level. Measure the space between the inside faces of the posts at the top and bottom—lines A and B—to make sure the distances are equal *(right)*.

If the ground slopes between the gateposts, keep your tape measure level when you measure the distance between posts: Mark a point near the bottom of one post and using a string and a water level, line level, or carpenter's level, mark a point on the other post level with the first mark. Measure between the marks. You'll find that this task is easier with a helper.

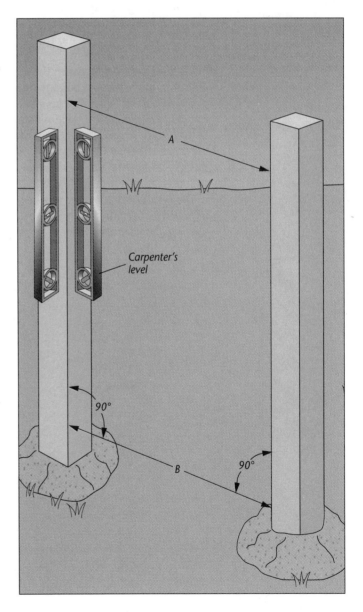

Carpenter's level

GATE FRAMES

The frame is the skeleton that supports the weight of a gate. So the type of frame you build will depend on both the size of the gate and the weight of the siding to be supported. Almost all gate frames need cross bracing to keep the gate square and prevent sagging; exceptions are gates with plywood or other rigid sheet siding. Bracing can be a diagonal piece of wood or a wire and turnbuckle assembly, as discussed opposite.

The step-by-step sequence starting below shows how to build a simple gate frame using 2x4 lumber and then how to attach siding to it. The type of frame illustrated here is suitable for gates up to 6 feet tall and 3 feet wide. The overall dimensions and the lumber sizes can be adapted to suit a number of gate designs, such as those discussed on page 26, but keep in mind that larger gates will require heavier framing members.

Building a gate frame

TOOLKIT
- Tape measure
- Circular saw or crosscut saw
- Claw hammer
- Screwdriver (optional)
- Carpenter's square

1 ▸ Determining gate size
Plan the width of the frame to allow clearance space on both the hinge and latch sides of the gate, as shown at right. For gates with standard 2x4 framing and 4x4 posts, leave 1/2" between the latch post and the gate frame so the gate will swing without binding. The space on the hinge side will depend on the type of hinges you're using; for most standard hinges, 1/4" is sufficient.

Measure the space between the gate posts at the top and bottom. (If it varies more than 1/4", you'll have to compensate for it: Adjust the position of the hinges, or shim them; or adjust the frame.) Then, subtract 3/4" from this measurement (to allow for gate swing clearance) for the gate width.

The height of your gate will be determined by both the height of the opening and your gate design.

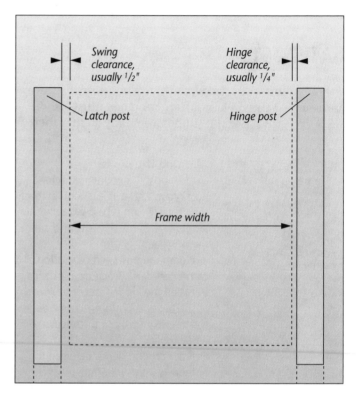

Swing clearance, usually 1/2"

Hinge clearance, usually 1/4"

Latch post

Hinge post

Frame width

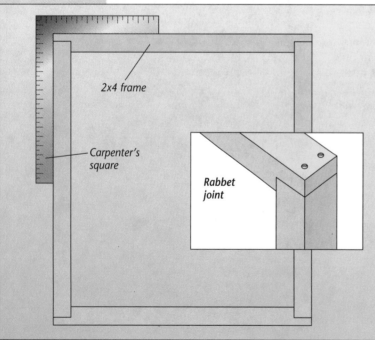

2x4 frame

Carpenter's square

Rabbet joint

2 ◂ Constructing the frame
Cut the frame pieces to length and assemble them on a work surface. You can butt the pieces together as you would fence rails and posts (page 48). But for a stronger joint, use rabbet joints (inset). Cut the rabbets—essentially dadoes, as shown on page 50, across the ends of a board—at both ends of the horizontal frame pieces.

For additional strength, fasten the pieces with wood screws and weatherproof yellow glue instead of nails. Whichever joinery method you choose, use a carpenter's square to confirm that the boards are perpendicular to each other as you join them (left).

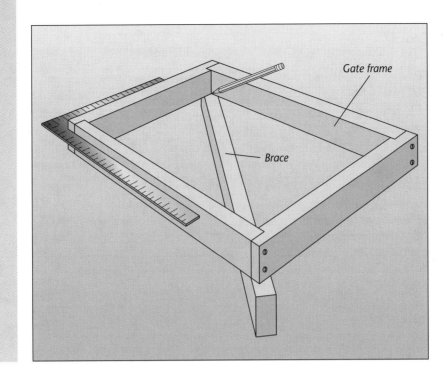

Gate frame

Brace

3 **Attaching a wood brace**

Set the gate frame on a 2x4 and mark the inside corners of the frame on the brace *(left)*. To get the tight fit required, saw the brace to length along the outside of the pencil marks.

Test-fit the brace in the frame and check that the corners remain at 90°; trim the ends of the brace, if necessary. Then attach the brace, nailing through both the horizontal and vertical frame pieces into the ends of the brace.

CHOICES FOR DIAGONAL BRACING

There are two standard ways to brace a gate. You can attach a board diagonally from the bottom of the hinge side to the top of the latch side *(below, left)*. This method is described above. Or, you can run a stainless steel cable or heavy wire and turnbuckle assembly from the bottom of the latch side to the top of the hinge side *(below, right)*. A wood brace is more likely to harmonize with your gate design than the wire and turnbuckle and will provide an additional nailing surface for wood siding. On the other hand, the turnbuckle assembly is easier to install, weighs less, and can be adjusted if the gate sags.

Cable or wire and turnbuckle assemblies are available at home centers; they are attached to the vertical members of the gate frame with large eye screws, as shown.

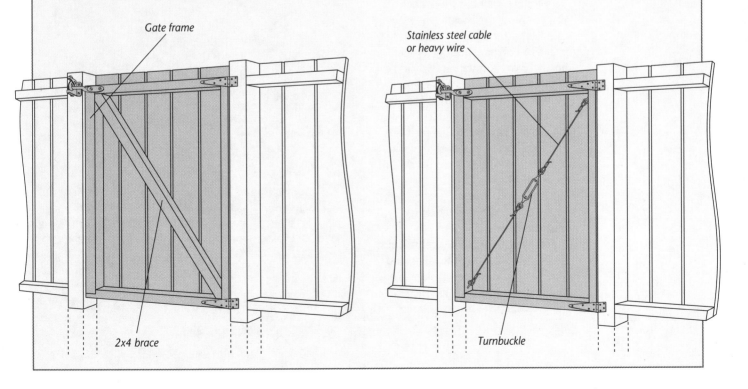

Gate frame

2x4 brace

Stainless steel cable or heavy wire

Turnbuckle

WHAT IF THE GROUND BETWEEN THE GATEPOSTS SLOPES?

If the ground slopes between the posts, you should still make a rectangular gate frame, ensuring that each of the four corners is at 90°. The bottom of the siding, rather than the bottom of the frame, can be angled.

When you apply the siding, you can cut it to follow the slope only if you hinge the gate on the downhill side (right). If you hinge the gate on the uphill side, cut the bottom of the siding so it won't scrape along the ground when the gate is opened.

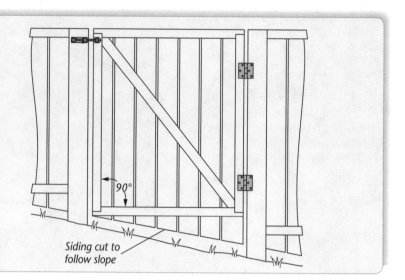

Siding cut to
follow slope

SIDING

Although the instructions presented below apply to attaching boards vertically to a gate frame, the procedures for installing horizontal or diagonal board sidings are not drastically different.

If the gate will be too heavy or awkward to lift with siding, you can apply the siding after the frame is hung, provided the hinges have been attached to the back side of the frame where they won't interfere.

Attaching siding

TOOLKIT
• Tape measure
• Circular saw or crosscut saw
• Plane (optional)
• Claw hammer
• Carpenter's square

Cutting and fastening the boards
Cut the boards or pickets to size and lay them vertically across the frame, starting flush with the edge on the hinge side; the last piece should be flush with the frame edge on the latch side. If not, you have three choices: You can space the boards slightly; you can use one additional board and plane a little from one edge of each board; or you can start at the middle with full-sized boards and cut or plane the two end boards to fit flush with the frame edges. NOTE: The siding can overlap the latch side if it acts as a gate stop, as described opposite.

Mark the position of the boards on the frame, then nail the pieces, starting at the hinge side; use a carpenter's square to check that each board is square to the frame.

For plywood or other sheet siding, lay the frame flat over the siding and trace the outside edges of the frame on the siding with a pencil. Then cut out the siding and nail it in place.

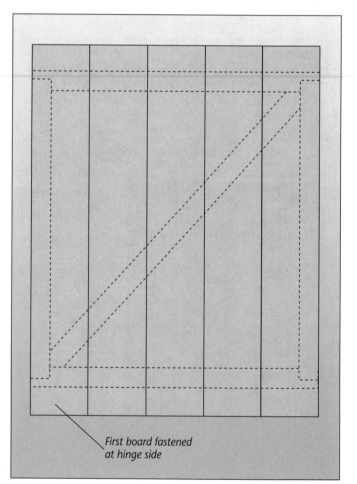

First board fastened
at hinge side

HANGING A GATE

Attaching hinges is the first step in hanging a gate. Your first concern should be the size of the fasteners: The screws should penetrate the frame and gatepost as far as possible without coming out the other side. You may find that the fasteners that come with the hinges are too short. If so, replace them with longer, corrosion-resistant screws.

You'll also need long screws for attaching the latch. Installation information for two common latch styles is given on page 58.

You can also install hardware to transform your gate into a sliding cantilever model. The hardware, which can also be used to convert an existing swing gate into a sliding one, is available in a kit.

Installing the gate

TOOLKIT
- Electric drill
- Screwdriver
- Plane
 (optional)

Fastening the hinges

Position each hinge on the gate, mark the screw holes, and drill a pilot hole at each mark, using a bit that is slightly smaller than the diameter of the fasteners. Attach the hinges to the gate.

Once the hinges are on, hold the gate in place to check the fit. If it's too close to the posts to swing freely, plane the edge of the latch side as needed. Then, either have a helper hold the gate in place or prop it in position with wood blocks, and mark the hinge screw holes on the post. Remove the gate and drill pilot holes; then reposition the gate and fasten the hinges to the post.

Once the gate is hung, make sure it swings easily, opens all the way, and closes flush with the posts; make any adjustments necessary. To help the gate close properly, you can install a spring (page 34).

The next step is to install the latch assembly on the gate and post (page 58). Use screws or bolts that are as long as possible without penetrating the other side.

Installing a gate stop

TOOLKIT
- Tape measure
- Circular saw
 or crosscut saw
- Claw hammer

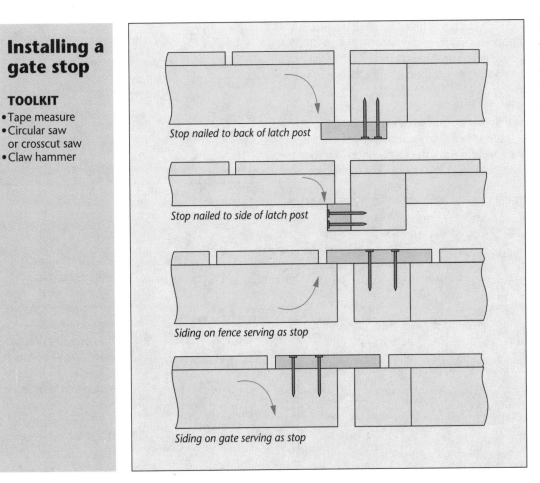

Stop nailed to back of latch post

Stop nailed to side of latch post

Siding on fence serving as stop

Siding on gate serving as stop

Postioning the stop

A gate stop is a vertical strip of wood attached to the latch post or gate to stop the gate when it closes; this keeps it from swinging past its closed position and loosening its hinges. The stop can be attached to the back or side of the latch post. The siding on the fence or gate can also serve as a stop by overlapping the gate frame or gatepost on the latch side. These possibilities are illustrated at left.

Cut a strip of lumber to the height of the gate; you can use 1x1, 1x2, 1x4, or 2x2 lumber, depending on the proportions of your gate and the location of the stop. Nail the stop to the post at the desired position.

CAN I BUILD A GATE IN PLACE?

Some builders actually prefer to build the gate in place, especially if a post is misaligned. Follow these steps:
1. Cut the horizontal pieces (rails) long enough to fit flush between the posts, and toenail them to the posts, leaving the nailheads protruding so you can remove the nails later.
2. Fasten the vertical pieces to the rails, placing plywood spacers between the posts and vertical pieces to provide the required clearance.

3. Cut and fasten the brace, making sure its bottom is on the hinge side.
4. Install face-mounted hinges, using the longest screws that won't break through the far side.
5. Nail the siding to the frame.
6. Remove the temporary nails and saw off the rails flush with the uprights.
7. Install the latch.

Installing a gate latch

TOOLKIT

• Tape measure
• Electric drill
• Keyhole saw or compass saw (optional)
• Screwdriver

Positioning a thumb latch

Measure from the edge of the gate to where the hole for the thumbpiece will go. The hole must be long enough to enable the bar to clear the strike plate's notch when the thumbpiece is raised. Mark the top and bottom of the hole on the gate, drill holes at these marks, and use a keyhole saw or compass saw to cut out the wood between the holes.

Next, slip the thumbpiece through the hole, hold the handle against the front of the fence, and mark the screw holes in the handle onto the fence. Remove the handle, drill pilot holes for the screws and then fasten the handle in place.

Now, position the bar and faceplate on the gate and mark the screw holes. Remove the pieces, drill pilot holes, and screw the bar and plate to the gate. If necessary, fasten a wood block to the gate behind the pivoting end of the bar so you'll have something to screw it to.

Finally, position the strike plate against the gate with the bar in its notch and resting on the bottom of the faceplate slot. Holding the plate in place, open the gate and mark the screw holes. Remove the plate, drill pilot holes, and fasten it to the gate *(right)*.

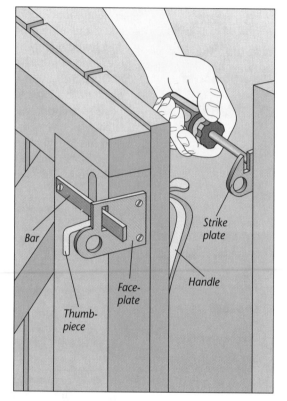

Bar

Thumb-piece

Face-plate

Strike plate

Handle

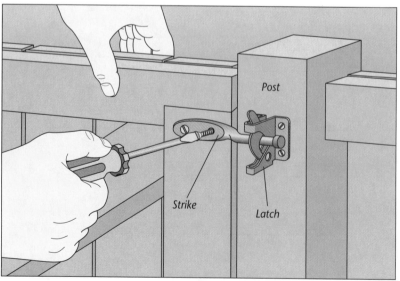

Post

Strike

Latch

Positioning a self-closing latch

Hold the latch in place on the post and mark the screw holes. Remove the latch, drill pilot holes, and fasten the latch in place. Next, insert the strike into the latch and mark the screw holes on the gate. Remove the strike, drill pilot holes, and screw the strike to the rail *(left)*.

POST-AND-RAIL FENCES

Homesteaders originally built split rail fences in a zigzag pattern, stacking the rails on top of each other and supporting the bottom on rocks. As trees became scarcer and property lines more exact, fence builders straightened out the zigzag pattern by stacking rails between paired posts. These double post-and-rail fences still required a considerable amount of wood and eventually people began to build fences with fewer rails, mortising them into single posts. One variation on the mortised post-and-rail fence, commonly available as prefabricated fencing, uses two or three 6-inch-diameter poles, often with tapered ends, mortised into square or round posts. To find split rails, look in the Yellow Pages under "Fence Materials." Common split rail lengths are 6, 7, and 8 feet; they vary in width, thickness, and shape.

A more formal look can be achieved with a post-and-rail fence by using dimension lumber. For color photos of post-and-rail fences, turn to page 5.

FORMAL POST-AND-RAIL

For a more formal post-and-rail fence, you can use standard dimensioned 4x4 rails set between 4x4 posts, as shown below. You can either dado and toe-nail the rails into the posts, as shown, or just toenail them between the posts. For a variation, rotate the rails 45° and toenail them between the posts.

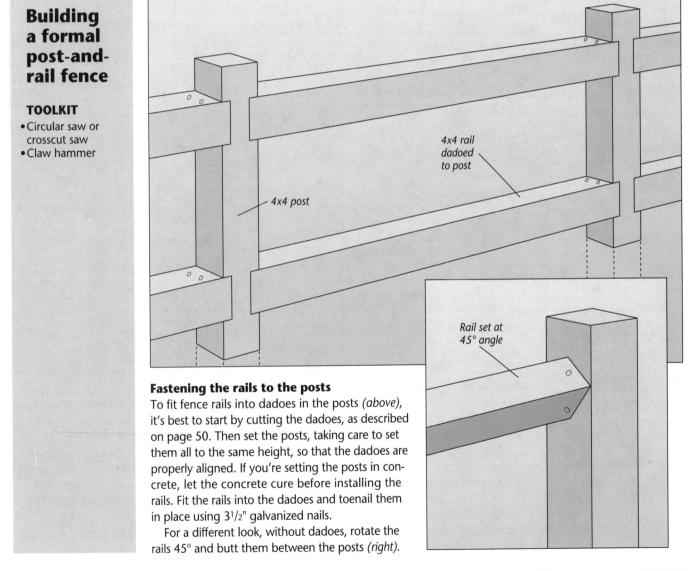

Building a formal post-and-rail fence

TOOLKIT
- Circular saw or crosscut saw
- Claw hammer

4x4 rail dadoed to post

4x4 post

Rail set at 45° angle

Fastening the rails to the posts
To fit fence rails into dadoes in the posts *(above)*, it's best to start by cutting the dadoes, as described on page 50. Then set the posts, taking care to set them all to the same height, so that the dadoes are properly aligned. If you're setting the posts in concrete, let the concrete cure before installing the rails. Fit the rails into the dadoes and toenail them in place using 3¹/₂" galvanized nails.

For a different look, without dadoes, rotate the rails 45° and butt them between the posts *(right)*.

MORTISED POST-AND-RAIL

There are a number of ways to mortise rails into posts, depending on the relative sizes and shapes of the posts and rails. Two of the more common methods are described here: overlapping the rails or cutting tenons into the rail ends. The fence shown at right features 6-foot-long rectangular posts, roughly 5 inches by 6 inches thick. The split rails shown are roughly 3 inches by 4 inches thick and about 6 to 8 feet long.

You'll need to plot the fence line and mark out the locations of the posts as described beginning on page 39. The distance between posts will depend both on the length of the rails and on the method you choose (overlap or mortise-and-tenon, as illustrated below) for mortising the rails into the posts.

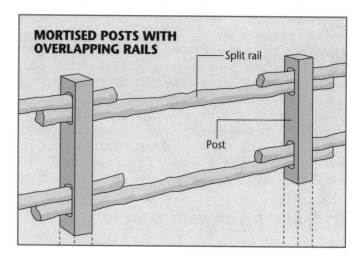

MORTISED POSTS WITH OVERLAPPING RAILS

Split rail

Post

Building a mortised post-and-rail fence

TOOLKIT
- Electric drill
- Butt chisel
- Mallet

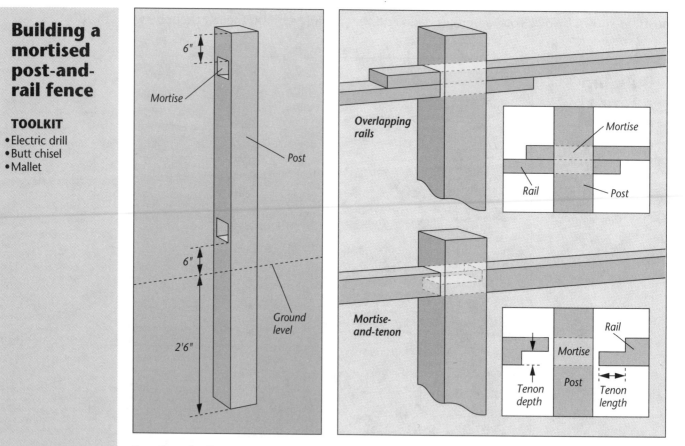

6"

Mortise

Post

6"

Ground level

2'6"

Overlapping rails

Mortise

Rail

Post

Mortise-and-tenon

Rail

Mortise

Tenon depth

Post

Tenon length

Erecting the fence

Cut mortises through the wide faces of the posts before setting them *(page 51)*; the mortises should start 6" above the ground and 6" below the top of the posts *(above, left)*. Be sure to set all the posts to the same height, so the rails will be level.

The size of the mortises depends on the width and thickness of the rails and the mortising method you're using. Overlapping rails require twice as much room as tenoned ones. If you're using mortise-and-tenons, the length of the tenons should equal the thickness of the post and the tenon depth should equal half the rail thickness *(above, right)*. At ends and corners, cut a blind mortise in the post and slip the rail in without cutting a tenon.

Set the first post *(page 42)* 2'6" deep and slip the rails into their mortises. Then have a helper insert the other ends of the rails into the mortises of the next post as you set it in place. Complete the fence one section at a time. For extra stability, you can nail through the post into the tenon.

POST-AND-BOARD FENCES

A familiar sight along many a country road, the post-and-board fence has traditionally been used to enclose large acreages. Among the easiest to build, these fences use perhaps the least amount of lumber of any wood fence. At today's lumber prices, the cost of rimming even an acre or two, using any other style of fence, can be prohibitive. But of course, post-and-board fences are attractive on any size lot.

The typical post-and-board fence is 3 to 4 feet high and has three rails, usually 1x4s or 1x6s, attached to the sides of the posts and running parallel with the ground.

But these fences accommodate a number of design variations, three of which are shown below. Some of these serve purposes other than simply adding visual interest to the fence. For example, post-and-board designs featuring closely spaced boards or alternating boards and slats will keep toddlers and pets from slipping through the fence, and the top and side details for posts shown on page 62 will help protect the fence from the weather. Taller versions (4 to 6 feet tall) are used for containing livestock and for horse corrals. Sturdier designs, such as those used to pen livestock, may have 2x6 rails. Lower versions (2½ to 4 feet tall) are often seen in the front yards of ranch-style houses or country estates. Post-and-board fences adapt especially well to hillsides and rolling terrain.

The sizes of the posts and boards you use will depend on your fence design. Ordinarily, if post spacing is 6 feet or less, use 4x4 lumber for square posts, or round posts 4 inches in diameter. For posts spaced over 6 feet apart, use square 6x6 posts or round posts 6 inches in diameter. Use boards twice the length of the post spacing so that you can stagger the joints on alternate posts, as shown on page 62.

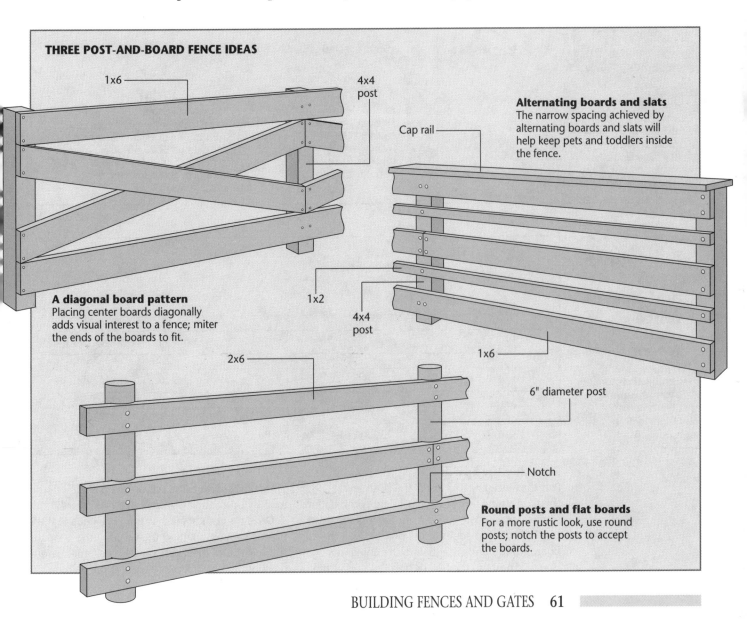

THREE POST-AND-BOARD FENCE IDEAS

1x6

4x4 post

Cap rail

Alternating boards and slats
The narrow spacing achieved by alternating boards and slats will help keep pets and toddlers inside the fence.

1x2

4x4 post

1x6

A diagonal board pattern
Placing center boards diagonally adds visual interest to a fence; miter the ends of the boards to fit.

2x6

6" diameter post

Notch

Round posts and flat boards
For a more rustic look, use round posts; notch the posts to accept the boards.

PROTECTING YOUR FENCE: TOP AND SIDE DETAILS

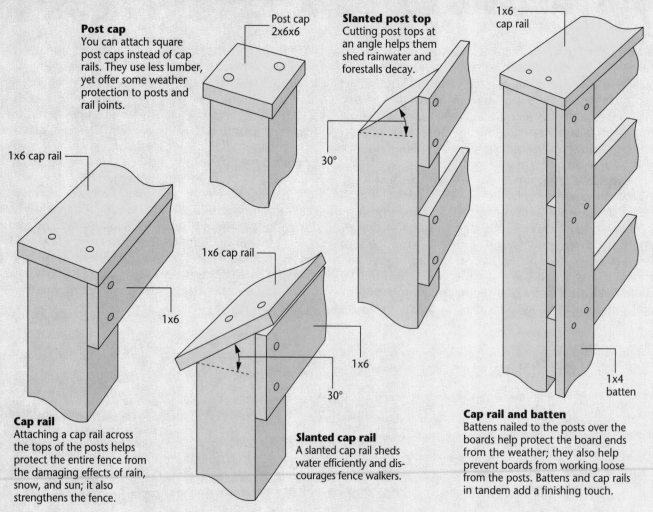

Post cap
You can attach square post caps instead of cap rails. They use less lumber, yet offer some weather protection to posts and rail joints.

Post cap 2x6x6

Slanted post top
Cutting post tops at an angle helps them shed rainwater and forestalls decay.

30°

1x6 cap rail

1x6 cap rail

1x6

Cap rail
Attaching a cap rail across the tops of the posts helps protect the entire fence from the damaging effects of rain, snow, and sun; it also strengthens the fence.

1x6 cap rail

1x6

30°

Slanted cap rail
A slanted cap rail sheds water efficiently and discourages fence walkers.

1x4 batten

Cap rail and batten
Battens nailed to the posts over the boards help protect the board ends from the weather; they also help prevent boards from working loose from the posts. Battens and cap rails in tandem add a finishing touch.

Building a post-and-board fence

TOOLKIT
- Tape measure
- Combination square or try square
- Claw hammer
- Electric drill (optional)

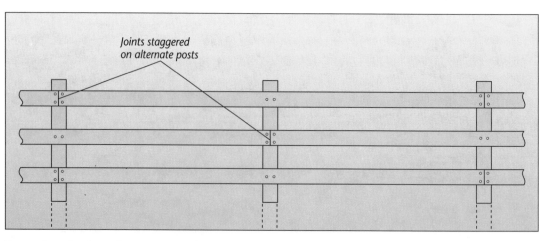

Joints staggered on alternate posts

Fastening the boards

Plot the fence line and install the posts *(page 39)*, then use a tape measure, pencil, and combination square or try square to mark lines across the posts to locate the top edges of the boards. Nail the boards to the posts, staggering the end joints on alternate posts so the boards don't all end at the same post *(above)*. Use galvanized nails: 2 1/2" nails for 1-by boards and 3 1/2" nails for 2-by boards.

Drive the nails at least 1" from the ends of the boards to avoid splitting the wood. If the boards still split, blunt the nail tips with a hammer before driving them or drill pilot holes for the nails.

PICKET FENCES

Traditionally, the picket fence has been associated with colonial architecture, but today it's found with almost any type of house, whether in the city or in the country. The wide range of picket and post top treatments available allow you to give your fence an individual character while keeping within the boundaries of traditional design. A few of these treatments are shown below.

The classic picket fence shown is about 3 feet high, with 4x4 posts spaced 6 feet on center and 2x4 rails butted between them. Overall post length is 5 feet (3 feet above ground and 2 feet below). Pickets are usually 1x3s spaced 2¹/₂ inches apart, though other sizes and spacings may be used *(page 64)*. Lumber dealers and fence suppliers don't always carry ready-made pickets, but you may have better luck at home centers. Many dealers will, however, cut boards to length, usually for a small fee.

You may want to cut the picket top designs yourself or have a cabinet shop or woodworker do the work. The latter choice may be preferable if you have many pickets to cut or if the design you want is an intricate one. For post tops, you'll probably want to have a complex design cut by an experienced woodworker, rather than doing it yourself, if the pattern you want is not available precut at a home center. For both pickets and posts, take the woodworker a sample piece with the top design traced on it in pencil. It's usually a good idea to get estimates from more than one shop for the work you want done.

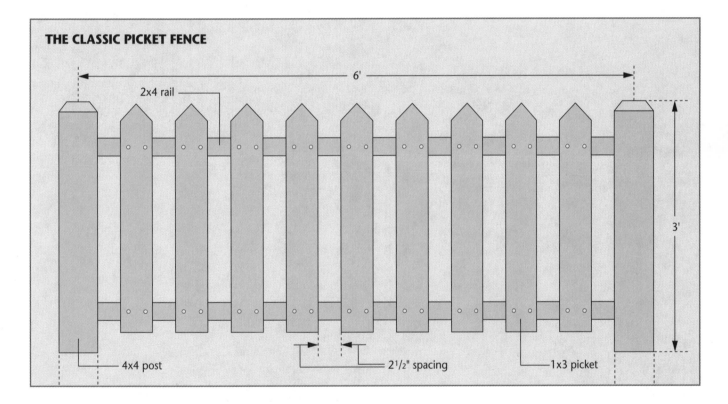

THE CLASSIC PICKET FENCE

6'

2x4 rail

3'

4x4 post

2¹/₂" spacing

1x3 picket

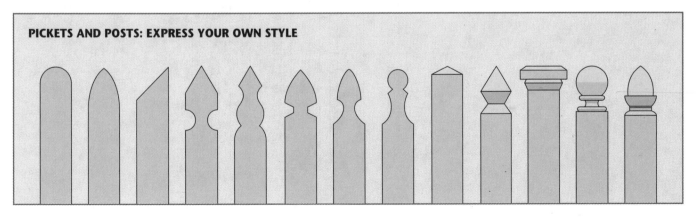

PICKETS AND POSTS: EXPRESS YOUR OWN STYLE

PICK YOUR FAVORITE PICKETS: FOUR FENCE STYLES

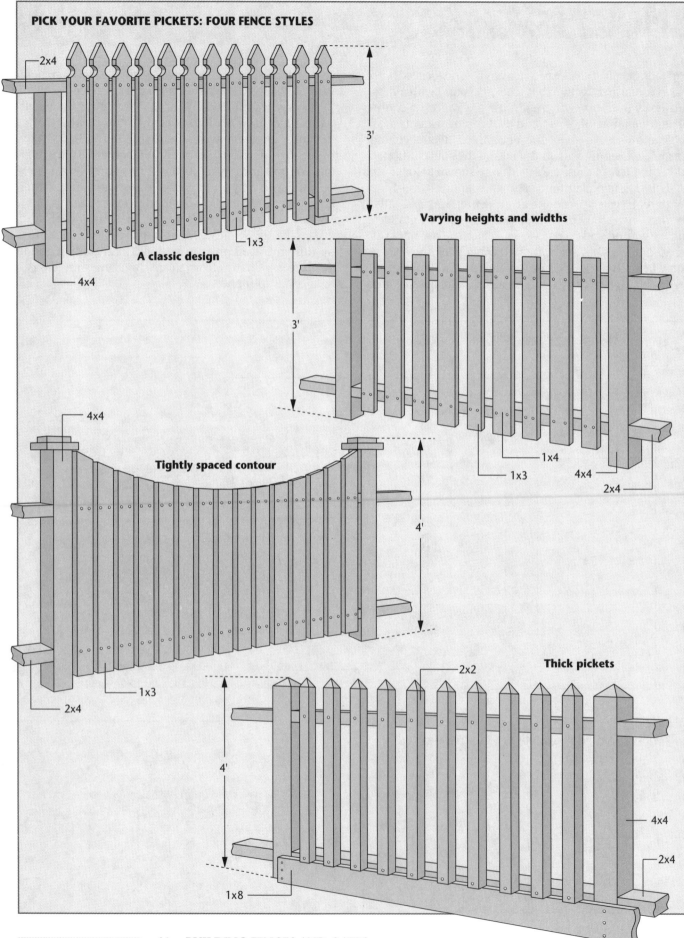

A classic design

Varying heights and widths

Tightly spaced contour

Thick pickets

2x4

1x3

4x4

3'

3'

1x4

1x3

4x4

2x4

4x4

2x4

1x3

4'

2x2

4'

1x8

4x4

2x4

Building a picket fence

TOOLKIT
- Circular saw or crosscut saw (optional)
- Saber saw (optional)
- C-clamp (optional)
- Claw hammer

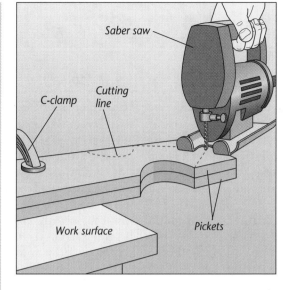

Saber saw

C-clamp

Cutting line

Work surface

Pickets

1 ▶ Cutting the pickets
Plot the fence line and lay out post locations *(page 39)*. Next, saw the pickets and posts to length, if necessary, then cut the picket tops and, if your design calls for it, the post tops as well.

If you're cutting your own pickets, lay them flat on a work surface to do the cutting. For simple pointed pickets, you can use either a circular saw or handsaw; for more intricate designs, use a saber saw. After you've cut the first picket, use it as a pattern for marking the rest.

To save time, you can cut two pickets at once (three, with a circular saw) by securing them together with C-clamps *(left)*, making sure the ends and edges of the boards are perfectly aligned.

2 ▶ Installing the posts and rails
Once all the pickets and post tops are cut, install the posts *(page 42)* and the rails *(page 48)*. To toenail 2x4 rails to 4x4 posts, use 3" galvanized nails.

If you decide to add a kickboard along the bottom of the fence *(page 52)*, nail it to the sides of the posts so that the pickets rest on top of it *(right)*. Since the kickboard will be in contact with the ground, make it of redwood or cedar heartwood or pressure-treated lumber.

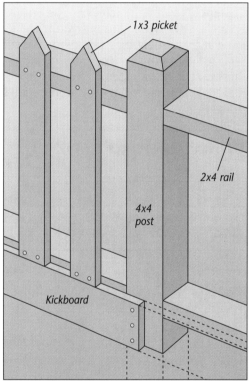

1x3 picket

2x4 rail

4x4 post

Kickboard

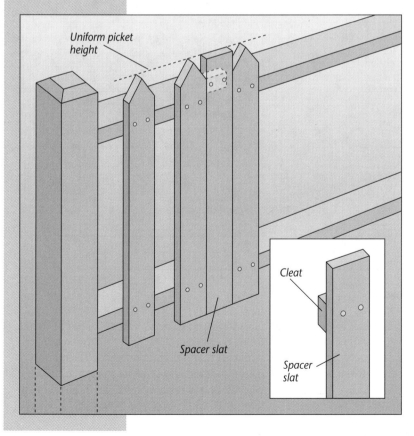

Uniform picket height

Spacer slat

Cleat

Spacer slat

3 ◀ Installing the pickets
To calculate the spacing between pickets, multiply the number of pickets you want between the posts by the width of the pickets. Subtract this number from the number of inches between the posts, then divide the resulting number by the number of spaces (the number of pickets plus one). Rip a picket to this width, to use as a spacer slat. Attach a small cleat to the back face *(inset)* so that when hung on the top rail, the top end of the slat is level with the tops of the pickets. Place the slat flush against the post, then butt a picket against it. Align the bottom of the picket with the slat and nail the picket in place using 2 1/4" galvanized nails *(left)*. Reposition the slat and repeat the process.

BOARD FENCES

Board fences are easy to build, but they must be thoughtfully designed and located to overcome a number of disadvantages. Solid-board fences are expensive because they require a great deal of lumber. Furthermore, although they offer maximum privacy, they can create a boxed-in feeling. Before you choose a style, refer to the chapter on planning *(page 17)* and decide what you want your fence to do. Some board fence variations are illustrated opposite.

Designs featuring boards nailed to one side of the frame will result in a fence with a front side and a back side. If you can talk your neighbor into sharing the cost of the fence, you might agree on a design that alternates the panels. Otherwise, you may want to face the front side toward your neighbor's property as a courtesy, with the frame side facing yours. There are a number of ways to dress up the frame side of a fence; some are discussed on page 80. The best solution is to design a board fence

that looks good on both sides; these are often referred to as "good neighbor fences."

The typical board fence *(below, left)* is 6 feet high, with a frame of 4x4 posts set 6 feet on center and 2x4 rails nailed between the posts. The posts are 8 feet long and are set 2 feet deep in the ground. To help support the weight of the boards, the bottom rail is sometimes placed on edge. Or you can install a kickboard *(page 52)*.

To add a little character to the basic board fence, you can cut the tops of the boards with one of several patterns *(below, right)*. It's easier to cut the board tops before attaching them to the fence and you can cut a few boards at a time as you would with pickets *(page 65)*.

In this section, we'll also show you how to build a louver fence (with either vertical or horizontal louvers), which provides privacy without completely blocking airflow, and a basketweave fence, which uses thinner siding material than a typical board fence.

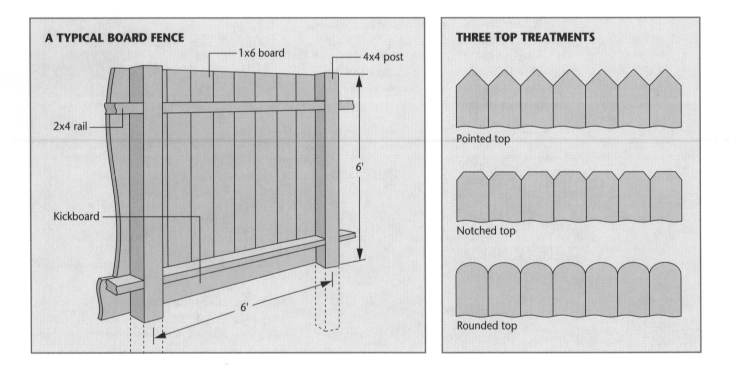

A TYPICAL BOARD FENCE

1x6 board   4x4 post

2x4 rail

6'

Kickboard

6'

THREE TOP TREATMENTS

Pointed top

Notched top

Rounded top

Building a board fence

TOOLKIT
- Claw hammer
- Carpenter's level for horizontal siding

1 Installing the posts, rails, and kickboard

Plot the fence line and lay out post locations *(page 39)*. Then install the posts *(page 42)* and join the rails to them *(page 48)*.

If you plan to install kickboards along the bottom of the fence to close the gap between the fence and the ground, use 1-by or 2-by lumber.

As shown on page 52, kickboards may be nailed to the undersides of the bottom rails or face-nailed to the posts and bottom rails; face-nailing is the easiest method and provides the siding boards with support. Use galvanized nails three times as long as the thickness of the kickboards.

2 Attaching the boards

For directions on attaching vertical siding, turn to page 52. You may need to leave a slight gap between boards to allow for expansion and contraction.

To attach horizontal siding, start with the bottom board. Position the board and fasten one end with a single nail. Place a carpenter's level on top of the board and adjust the board until it is level, then finish nailing it to the posts and rail. This will help ensure that successive boards will also be level.

Whether you're attaching siding vertically or horizontally, use galvanized nails three times as long as the thickness of the boards.

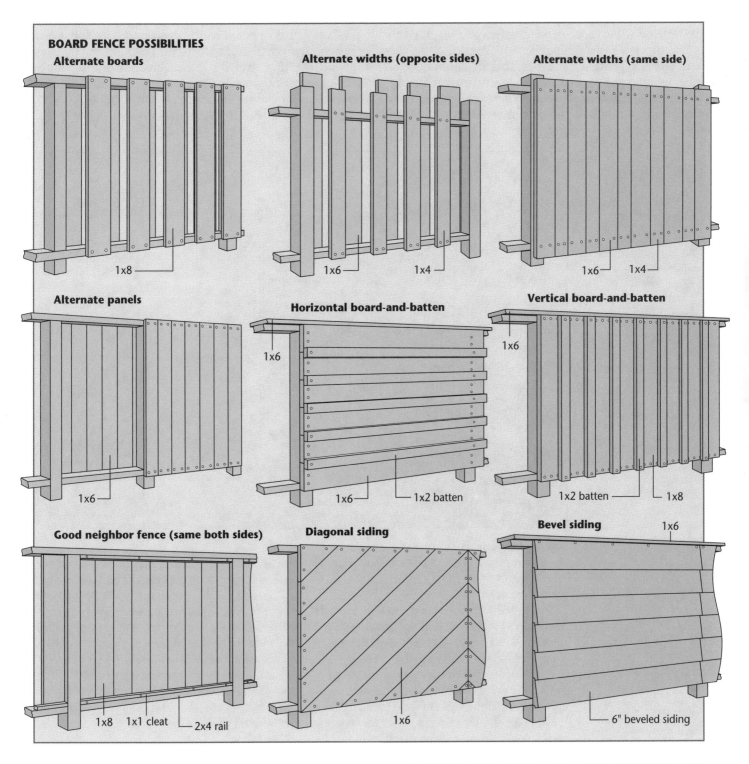

BOARD FENCE POSSIBILITIES

Alternate boards
1x8

Alternate widths (opposite sides)
1x6   1x4

Alternate widths (same side)
1x6   1x4

Alternate panels
1x6

Horizontal board-and-batten
1x6   1x6   1x2 batten

Vertical board-and-batten
1x6   1x2 batten   1x8

Good neighbor fence (same both sides)
1x8   1x1 cleat   2x4 rail

Diagonal siding
1x6

Bevel siding
1x6   6" beveled siding

LOUVER FENCES

The advantage of louver fences is that they provide privacy without substantially restricting the airflow through a yard or garden. Depending on the direction (vertical or horizontal), spacing, and angle of the louvers, you can control the amount of sunlight on plants near the fence and temper harsh winds, yet limit or completely block the view from outside into a yard.

Vertical louvers offer relative privacy—only a small portion of the yard is fully visible to anyone walking past. Horizontal louvers placed with their blind side toward the outside allow those inside the fence to see out, but block the view from the public side. To provide privacy with either type of louver fence, the edge of one louver must overlap the edge of the next one.

Louver fences are relatively expensive because they require more material per running foot than a solid board fence of the same height. Louvers should be made of kiln-dried lumber to minimize warping and sagging. Above average carpentry skills are needed to ensure that the fence parts fit properly. Needless to say, these fences should be used in fairly short runs and placed judiciously to take full advantage of their benefits.

The two louver fences discussed below are 6 feet tall with louvers set at a 45° angle. Posts are 8-foot-long 4x4s, set 2 feet deep, 4 feet on center. The top rails are 8-foot-long 2x4s that span three posts, and the bottom rails are 2x4s cut to fit between the posts and then toenailed between the posts. The spacers are 1x4 lumber.

For the vertical style, the louvers are 1x6s slightly under 5 feet long; for the horizontal louver fence, the louvers are 1x6s as long as the bottom rails. On either fence, you can fasten kickboards to the bottom rails and posts.

Building a vertical louver fence

TOOLKIT
- Tape measure
- Combination square
- Circular saw or crosscut saw
- Adjustable T-bevel
- Claw hammer

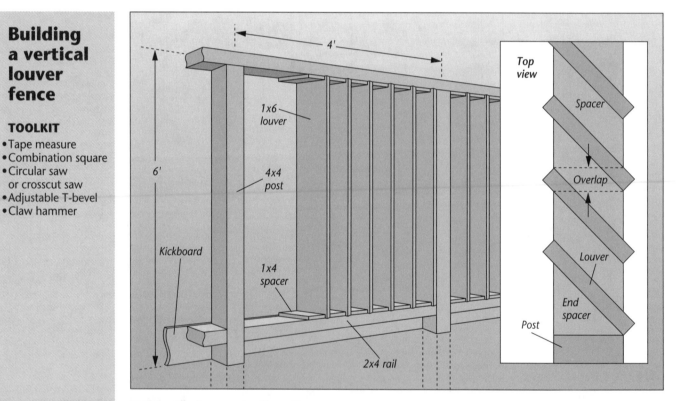

Nailing the louvers to the rails

Plot the fence line and lay out post locations *(page 39)*. Then install the posts *(page 42)* and join the rails to them *(page 48)*.

To determine the height of the louvers, measure the distance between the top and bottom rails and subtract 1/8"; for accuracy, make the measurements along the inside faces of the posts.

Cut the louvers, then cut a pair of spacers from 1x4 lumber to fit between two louvers *(inset)*, keeping in mind that the louvers should overlap. Check the fit of the spacers, make any necessary adjustments, and cut the remaining spacers.

Cut a pair of end spacers, one for the top and one for the bottom, to fit between the post and the first louver, and nail the spacers to the rails flush against the post. Position the first louver against both spacers and toenail it into the rails. Butt spacers (shaped like those in the inset) against the louver, top and bottom, and nail them to the rails. Add another louver and repeat the process *(above)*. When you get to the other post, cut two more spacers to fit between the louvers and the post, and nail them in place. Use galvanized nails three times as long as the thickness of the louvers.

TOOLKIT
- Tape measure
- Combination square
- Circular saw or crosscut saw
- Adjustable T-bevel
- Claw hammer

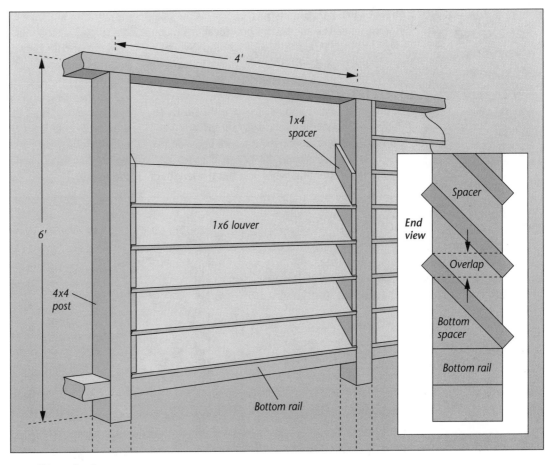

Installing the louvers

Plot the fence line *(page 39)*, lay out post locations *(page 42)*, and install the posts and rails *(page 48)* as for vertical louvers.

Cut the louvers to fit between the posts, then measure and cut one pair of 1x4 spacers to fit between two louvers *(inset)*, keeping in mind that the louvers must overlap each other. Check that the spacers fit properly, adjust their dimensions if necessary, and cut the remaining spacers.

Cut two triangular spacers to fit between the bottom rail and the first louver, again starting with one pair and checking for fit; you'll need spacers of this shape for each section of the fence, at both the top and bottom. Nail these spacers to two consecutive posts flush against the bottom rail. Position the first louver against the spacers and toenail it into the posts. Then butt spacers against the louver at both ends and nail them to the posts. Add another louver and repeat the process *(above)*. Use galvanized nails three times as long as the thickness of the louvers.

BASKETWEAVE FENCES

This type of fence is a popular project for do-it-yourselfers because it's easy to construct, requires a minimum of materials for a solid barrier, and, when completed, has a pleasing interwoven design with attractive shadow patterns. Instructions for building two basic designs—the horizontal basketweave and the vertical basketweave—are given on the next page.

Because the strips must be relatively thin to permit weaving, this fence often works better in mild climates; harsh weather can rapidly deteriorate the wood. The horizontal version should be avoided if there are potential fence climbers about—it makes a perfect stepladder, and climbing damages the wood strips.

The two fences shown are 6 feet tall. The 4x4 posts are 8 feet long and set 2 feet underground, 4 feet on center. The top rails are 8-foot-long 2x4s, each spanning three posts; the bottom rails are 2x4s cut long enough to fit between the posts, then toenailed in place. The siding is wood strips 1/2 inch thick and 6 inches wide, nailed to 1x2 strips and fastened to either the post or the rails, depending on the version being built.

The vertical basketweave fence shown here has 2x2s toenailed to the posts midway between the top and bottom rails; the horizontal version has 1x1 spacers positioned midway between the posts around which the wood strips are woven.

Building a horizontal basket-weave fence

TOOLKIT
• Tape measure
• Combination square
• Circular saw or crosscut saw
• Claw hammer

Weaving the siding strips

Plot the fence line and lay out post locations *(page 39)*. Then install the posts *(page 42)* and join the rails to them *(page 48)*. You may prefer to leave the top rail off until you have finished weaving the fence.

Cut 1x2 nailing strips to fit between the top and bottom rails; center and nail them to the posts. To determine the length of the siding strips, cut one strip about 2" longer than the distance between two posts. Have a helper hold the 1x1 spacer vertically against the bottom rail while you test the length of the strip. Cut off about ¹/₄" at a time, from one end, until the strip fits between the posts when bent around the spacer. Use this strip as a guide for cutting the remaining ones.

Nail the siding strips to the 1x2s, alternating sides, as shown below. Finally, thread the 1x1 spacer through the strips, centering it between the posts to create a basketweave *(inset)*, and toenail it in place. If you've left the top rail off, fasten it in place after inserting the spacer.

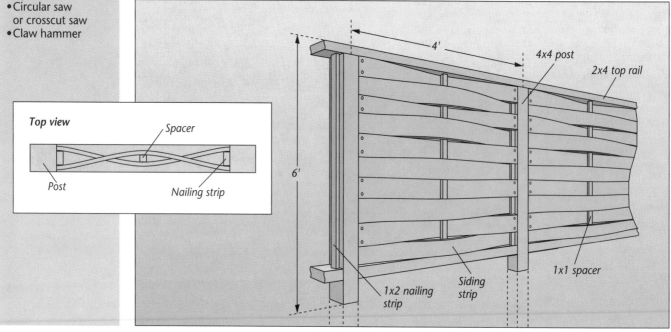

Top view

Spacer

Post

Nailing strip

4'

4x4 post

2x4 top rail

6'

1x2 nailing strip

Siding strip

1x1 spacer

Building a vertical basket-weave fence

TOOLKIT
• Tape measure
• Combination square
• Circular saw or crosscut saw
• Claw hammer

Constructing the fence

Plot the fence line, lay out post locations *(page 39)*, install the posts *(page 42)*, and join the rails to them *(page 48)*.

Measure the distance between posts and cut two 1x2 nailing strips to this length for each section. Center and nail the strips to the top and bottom rails. Cut a 2x2 spacer to the same length, and toenail it between the posts midway between the rails.

The siding strips must be long enough to be woven around the 2x2. Cut one strip about 2" longer than the distance between the rails, then cut off one end, ¹/₄" at a time, until the strip fits properly. Use it as a pattern for cutting the remaining strips.

Weave the siding strips around the 2x2s and fasten them to the nailing strips *(right)*. Finally, attach the strips to the spacer.

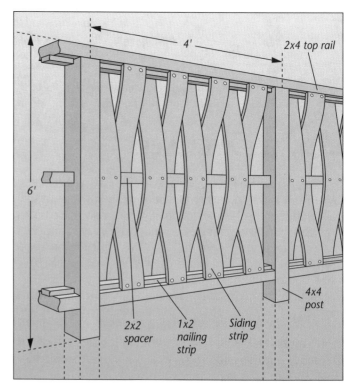

4'

2x4 top rail

6'

2x2 spacer

1x2 nailing strip

Siding strip

4x4 post

GRAPESTAKE FENCES

Rough-split redwood stakes, used for propping up grapevines in vineyards, have long been a popular material for making rustic-looking fences.

Grapestake fences are more common in the western United States than in other parts of the country because redwood stakes are more accessible in the West. Their counterpart east of the Rockies is the stockade fence, which uses round, pointed stakes 2 to 3 inches in diameter. Building methods for both fences are the same.

The most common type of grapestake fencing (illustrated on the next page) consists of stakes nailed vertically to the side of a standard fence frame of 4x4 posts and 2x4 rails. Left unpainted, the stakes will weather to a soft, silvery gray that provides a natural-looking backdrop for plantings, and complements the warm tones of brick and stonework in a garden.

As shown below, the versatile grapestake can be used to create a number of fence designs, high or low, formal

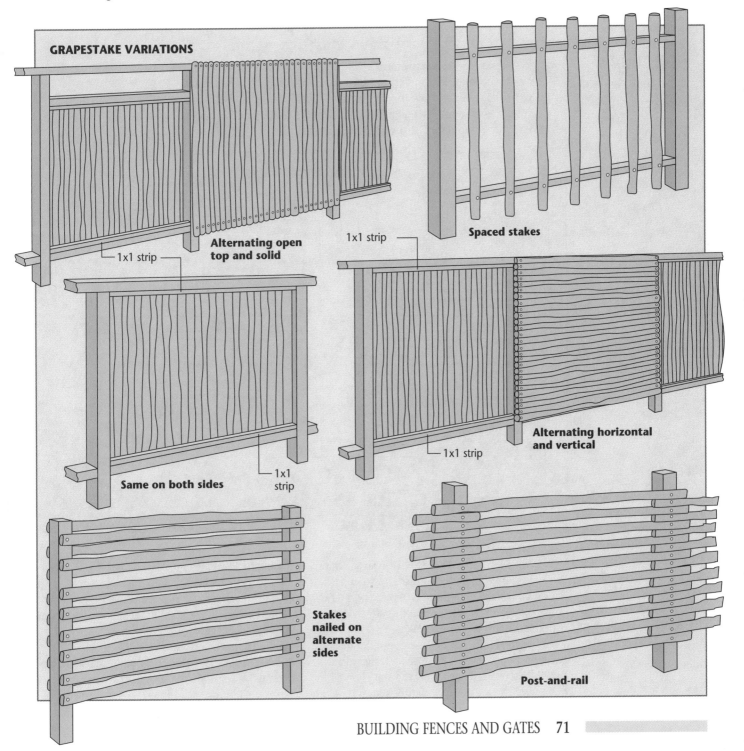

GRAPESTAKE VARIATIONS

1x1 strip

Alternating open top and solid

1x1 strip

Spaced stakes

1x1 strip

Same on both sides

1x1 strip

Alternating horizontal and vertical

1x1 strip

Stakes nailed on alternate sides

Post-and-rail

or informal. The narrow stakes are especially suitable for hillside *(page 24)* and curved fencing *(page 25)*.

Grapestakes are split from redwood logs, so they have irregular, splintery edges; it's best to wear work gloves when handling them. They were originally split from heartwood, but there is a trend today toward the use of sapwood, which has a tendency to decay rapidly when placed in the ground.

Grapestakes are available from 3 to 6 feet in length, either in the full 2-inch diameter size or, more commonly, as 1x2 slats cut lengthwise from 2x2 stock. The slats are more economical and easier to nail against flat rails.

There are some disadvantages to grapestake fences: Some people object to the splintery surface of the stakes;

and they're difficult to paint, so if you don't like the natural, weathered look of this type of fence, you might be disappointed. Solid grapestake fencing is also relatively expensive, and although the stakes are easy to handle, building the fence can become a tedious chore—keep in mind that 100 feet of solid grapestake fencing requires more nails than are needed to attach siding to a five-room house.

The fence shown below uses 4x4 posts cut 8 feet long and set 2 feet in the ground, 6 feet on center. The rails are 2x4s toenailed between the posts. Unless you're installing a kickboard *(page 52)*, use a 6-foot-long 1x4 to align the bottoms of the stakes. Use galvanized nails three times as long as the thickness of the grapestakes.

Building a grapestake fence

TOOLKIT
- Combination square
- Circular saw
- Claw hammer
- Tape measure (optional)
- Carpenter's level

1 Preparing the frame and stakes
Plot the fence line and lay out post locations *(page 39)*. Then install the posts *(page 42)* and join the rails to them *(page 48)*. Because of the weight of the grapestakes, you may want to set the bottom rail on edge to keep it from sagging. Cut the grapestakes to length.

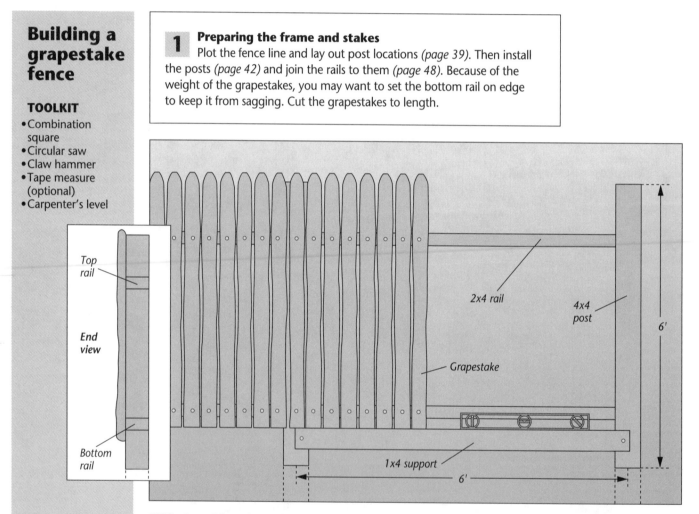

Top rail

End view

Bottom rail

2x4 rail

4x4 post

Grapestake

1x4 support

6'

6'

2 Attaching the stakes
When the frame is complete, begin attaching the stakes, starting at one end of the fence and nailing each stake to both rails. Depending on how you want the fence to look, you can attach stakes with the pointed end up or down.

Unless you're using a kickboard, temporarily nail a 6' long 1x4 support board between the posts at the bottom of the fence to rest the stakes on as you nail them. Use a 2' long carpenter's level to align the board so that the stake tops will line up level *(above)*. Nail the first stake to the rails, checking it with the level to make sure it's vertical.

Because grapestakes are irregular in shape, check with the level every fourth or fifth stake as you're nailing to make sure they're still vertical. If you find the stakes have started to slant, you can compensate by adjusting the tops or bottoms of a few stakes until they're all running vertically again.

LATTICE FENCES

Lattice screens and fences are light, airy structures, commonly associated with Victorian architecture. They can be used for several purposes in the yard: A tightly woven lattice can be used to screen out an objectionable view while allowing air to flow into the yard; widely spaced latticework can preserve a view, serve as a traffic director, or provide a backdrop for tall plantings. For more screen ideas, see page 78.

Latticework usually consists of thin lath, crisscrossed horizontally and vertically or diagonally, and held within a frame. Because of their light weight and open design, lattice fences and screens can be built as tall as 8 feet without requiring heavy framing members or bracing. The fence shown below is only one of many popular designs; for some other ideas, turn to the color photo section beginning on page 4.

The screen shown uses lath 1$\frac{1}{2}$ inches wide and $\frac{1}{4}$ inch thick. You'll need nine pieces 8 feet long and 17 pieces 65$\frac{1}{2}$ inches long for every 8 feet of screen. The posts are 2x4s, 8 feet long and set 2 feet in the ground, 4 feet on center. The top rails are 8-foot-long 2x4s nailed across three posts and the bottom rails are 2x4s cut to length to butt between the posts. Use galvanized nails three times as long as the thickness of the lath.

You can buy preassembled 4x8-foot lattice panels for which you can build a frame. Use posts about 6$\frac{1}{2}$ feet long and set them 2 feet deep, leaving 6 inches of space between the ground and the bottom of the panel.

Building a lattice fence

TOOLKIT
- Tape measure
- Backsaw and miter box
- Claw hammer
- Combination square

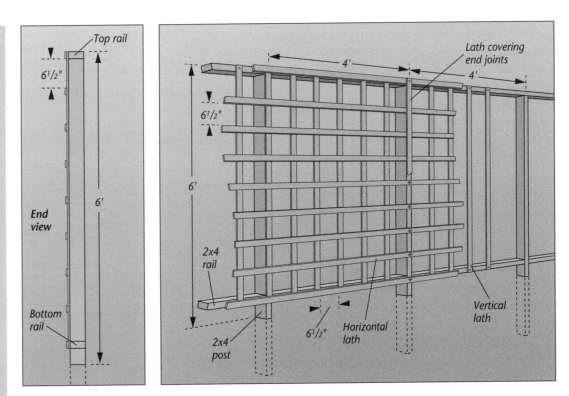

Attaching the strips

Plot the fence line and lay out post locations (*page 39*). Then install the posts (*page 42*) and join the rails to them (*page 48*). If you wish to paint the screen, it's easier to paint the frame and individual lath strips before joining them. Cut the lath strips to length, using a backsaw and miter box for square, clean cuts.

Attach the first vertical lath strip to the face of the first post. Space successive vertical strips 6$\frac{1}{2}$" apart, measuring and marking their locations on the top and bottom rails with a combination square and a pencil. Use one nail at the top and one at the bottom to attach each strip.

Once all of the vertical strips are nailed to the frame, attach the first horizontal strip along the face of the bottom rail, overlapping the vertical strips. Space successive horizontal strips 6$\frac{1}{2}$" apart, measuring and marking their locations on the posts. Use one nail at each end to attach the strips to the posts. The last strip should end up directly over the face of the top rail, as shown above.

When all of the horizontal strips are fastened, you may wish to protect the lath ends by nailing vertical strips over the joints. This will also help keep the lath ends from working loose.

PANEL FENCES

Fences and screens built with panels have several advantages over other types of fences. They can offer maximum privacy and provide a measure of wind protection. And once the fence frame is complete, panels can be quickly installed.

Plywood panels are available in different thicknesses and with a variety of finishes, such as smooth or rough-sawn (*page 30*); hardboard panels are also available. Both plywood and hardboard siding can be used to build a solid fence; you can buy it primed for improved weather resistance.

Panel fences require strong structural support, not only because of the weight of the materials, but also because a solid panel fence must withstand the force of the wind. Make sure that at least one third of the post length is in the ground and set in concrete. For the fence shown below, the posts are 4x4s with 2x4 rails butted between them; the bottom rail is made up of two 2x4s set on edge. To cover the edges of the

panels, 1x6 strips are used, but narrower strips (such as 1x2s) would also work. To fasten the panels to the fence frame, use galvanized nails three times as long as the panel thickness.

ASK A PRO

DO I NEED TO FINISH A WOOD PANEL FENCE?
No matter what type of panel you're using, whether exterior-grade plywood or primed hardboard siding, you should seal the faces and especially the edges with paint or another good exterior finish. Remember to paint the backs of the panels as well. You'll need to repaint your fence regularly. If you can design your fence so that plywood edges are protected from the weather (covered by strips of 1-by lumber, for example), so much the better.

Building a face panel fence

TOOLKIT
• Combination square
• Circular saw or crosscut saw
• Claw hammer
• Carpenter's level

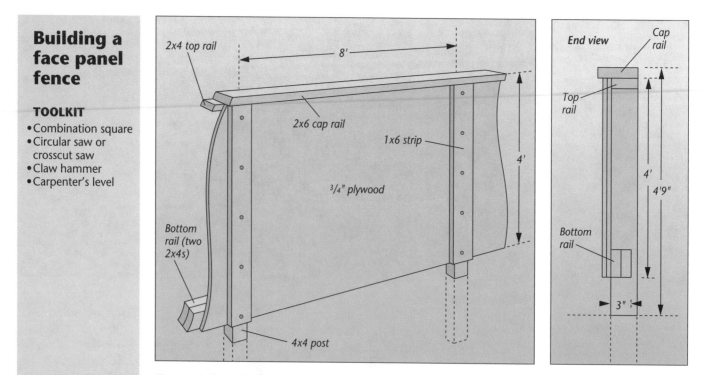

Constructing the fence
Plot the fence line, lay out post locations (*page 39*), and install the posts (*page 42*). Cut the rails to length, butt them between the posts and toenail them in place. For the bottom rail, set two 2x4s on edge, aligning them with the side of the fence to which you intend to attach the panel (*above, left*).

With a helper, hold the panel in place, check it for level, and nail it to the posts and the rails. Install the panels so that the joints between them fall in the center of the posts. When all of the panels are installed, nail strips of 1x6 lumber over the joints into the posts.

Finally, to help protect the panels from the weather, install a 2x6 cap rail over the tops of the panels, face-nailing it to the tops of the posts (*above, right*).

WOOD-AND-WIRE FENCES

Wire mesh has numerous applications in fencing. Heavy wire mesh provides security and offers support for plants without completely blocking a view. Chain-link fencing is popular for residential security.

Most wire and chain-link fences use metal posts and are best if professionally installed. However, instructions are given on the next page for a wood-and-wire fence that can easily be constructed by a do-it-yourselfer with the aid of a strong helper. This fence consists of 2x4 welded wire mesh attached to a wood frame of 4x4 posts and 2x4 rails. You can buy wire mesh in 50- and 100-foot rolls, and in a number of widths (3, 4, and 6 feet, for example); the width of the wire corresponds to the height of the fence. The fence shown here uses the 4-foot width, but you can adapt the design to a 3- or 6-foot fence. You might also want to substitute a tighter mesh or one of the patterns shown at right.

Fasten framing members with galvanized nails three times as long as the thickness of the wood. Use 3/4-inch galvanized staples to hold the wire to the posts and rails.

ASK A PRO

HOW CAN I GET MORE PRIVACY WITH A CHAIN-LINK FENCE?

If you want a chain-link fence, but you also want more privacy than the open design offers, you can create a solid fence by inserting slats of wood or plastic in the links; the slats are commercially available, specifically designed for this purpose. You can also buy slats made of wire and colored PVC that are designed to give your fence the appearance of a closely cropped hedge (page 15).

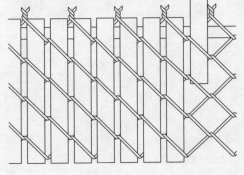

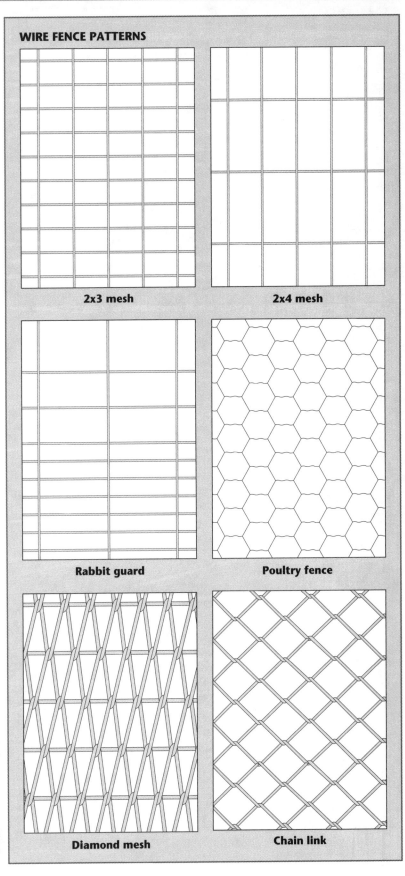

WIRE FENCE PATTERNS

2x3 mesh

2x4 mesh

Rabbit guard

Poultry fence

Diamond mesh

Chain link

TOOLKIT
- Tape measure
- Combination square
- Circular saw or crosscut saw
- Claw hammer
- Carpenter's level
- Diagonal-cutting pliers (wire-cutting pliers)

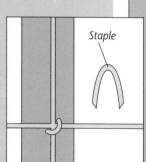

Staple

1 Preparing the frame

Plot the fence line and post locations *(page 39)*. Cut 6' lengths of 4x4s for the posts and set them 18" deep, 6' on center *(page 42)*. For the top rail, use 2x4s about 12' long (they'll span three posts); for the bottom rails, cut 2x4s to butt between the posts, level them, and toe-nail them in place.

Center a 1x6 cap rail over the top rail and nail it in place. You can cover the bottom edge of the wire with kickboards *(page 52)*.

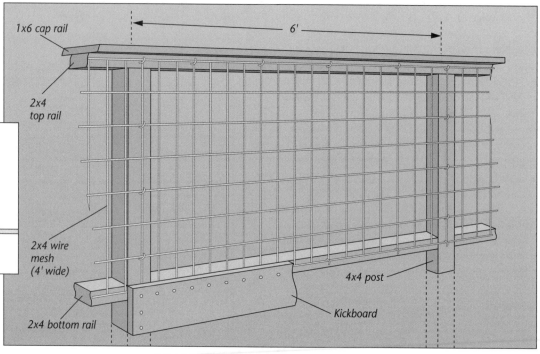

1x6 cap rail
6'
2x4 top rail
2x4 wire mesh (4' wide)
2x4 bottom rail
4x4 post
Kickboard

2 Attaching wire

Start at one end of the fence and unroll enough wire to cover two sections—about 12'. Align the top of the wire with the underside of the 1x6 cap rail.

Next, tack the wire to the first post, hammering staples at the top, center, and bottom. While a helper stretches the wire taut, tack the wire to the next two posts at the top, center, and bottom, checking frequently to make sure that it stays in alignment.

Once the wire is tacked in place over the first two sections, go back and secure it to the posts and rails by driving staples every 6". Fasten the staples as shown in the inset.

3 Completing the fence

Repeat the whole process until you reach the end of the fence. If you run out of wire before reaching the end of the fence, splice a new roll by overlapping the meshes on a post. Cut the old piece so that it ends at the edge of the post *(right, top)*. Lay the new piece on top of it, overlapping two vertical wires if possible. Fasten both pieces to the post with staples every 6" *(right, bottom)*.

Finally, fasten the kickboards to the bottom of the fence *(page 52)*. If you wish to give the fence a more finished appearance you can cover the staples by nailing 1x4 strips to the posts and 1x2 strips to the top rail.

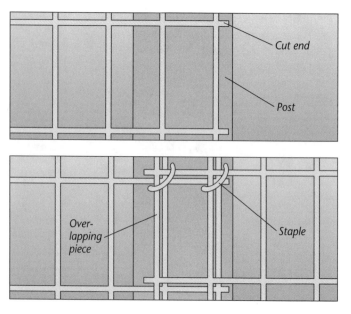

Cut end
Post
Over-lapping piece
Staple

LOW AND GARDEN FENCES

You may want to delineate a property line or an area on your property without the expense or even the appearance of a formal fence. And if you're plagued by people taking shortcuts across a part of your property, you can erect something simple across the path to discourage them. Some ideas for low fences, which can be used to direct traffic, clarify boundaries, or surround your garden, are illustrated below; they can all be built using the information in this chapter. If the fence must be strong, set the posts in concrete.

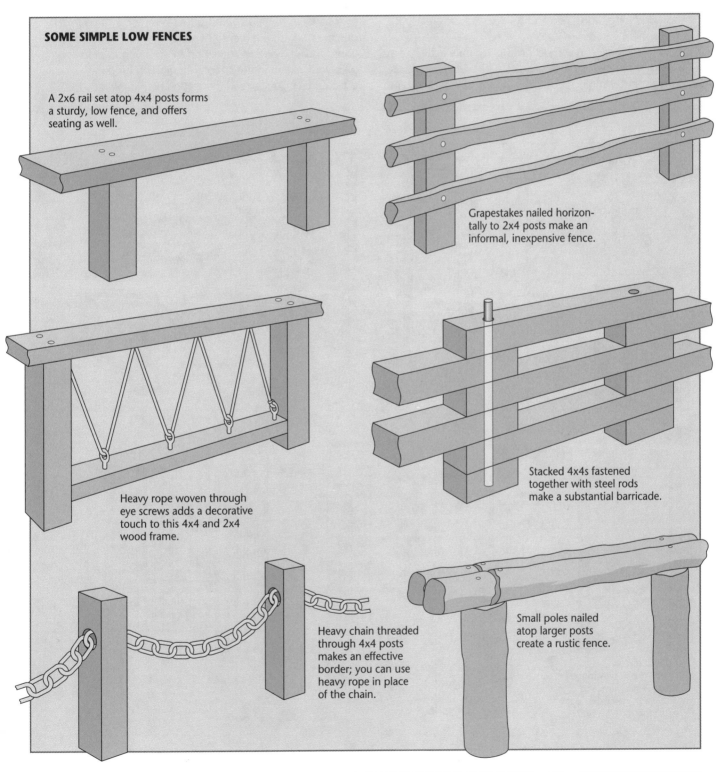

SOME SIMPLE LOW FENCES

A 2x6 rail set atop 4x4 posts forms a sturdy, low fence, and offers seating as well.

Grapestakes nailed horizontally to 2x4 posts make an informal, inexpensive fence.

Heavy rope woven through eye screws adds a decorative touch to this 4x4 and 2x4 wood frame.

Stacked 4x4s fastened together with steel rods make a substantial barricade.

Heavy chain threaded through 4x4 posts makes an effective border; you can use heavy rope in place of the chain.

Small poles nailed atop larger posts create a rustic fence.

GARDEN SCREENS

A screen is a short fence, often more lightly constructed than a full fence, erected within the bounds of a piece of property to provide privacy, shade, shelter from the wind, a backdrop for plants, a barrier, or decoration.

With imaginative design and proper placement of screens, you can create a private world on your property without a penned-in feeling. Choose from high and low, short and long, and open and solid screens to create the atmosphere you desire.

With screens, you can define and separate activity areas; provide privacy for parties, quiet gatherings, and other outdoor entertaining; control sunlight to create varying degrees of light and shade; provide protection from the wind; and create an illusion of quiet by visually blocking out sources of noise. You can also use screens to hide unsightly equipment and garbage storage areas, or to provide a background or support for plants or artwork.

Almost any type of fence shown in this book can be converted into a screen. The illustrations below offer some specific ideas to help you introduce a screen into your garden planning; the dimensions shown can be adjusted to fit your particular needs. You'll find information to help you plan your screen in the chapter beginning on page 17. For building techniques, read the section beginning on page 37.

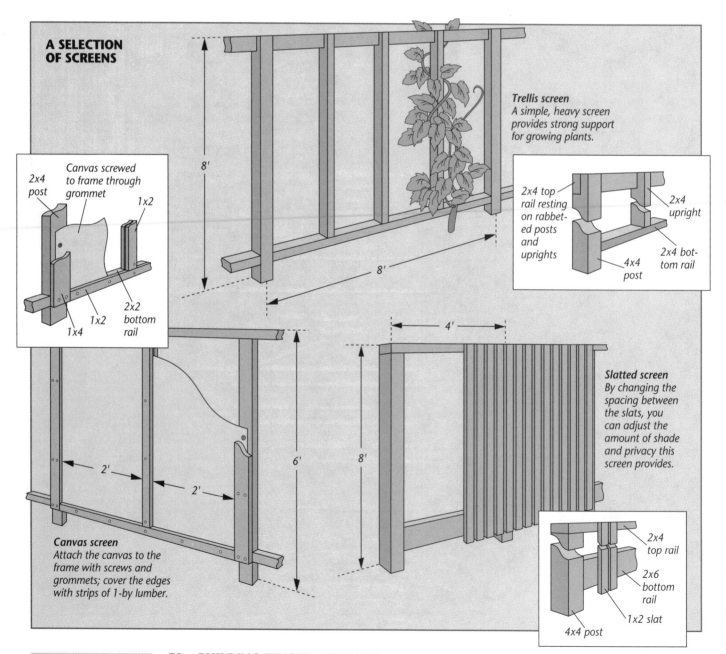

A SELECTION OF SCREENS

8'

8'

Trellis screen
A simple, heavy screen provides strong support for growing plants.

2x4 post

Canvas screwed to frame through grommet

1x2

1x2

1x4

2x2 bottom rail

2x4 top rail resting on rabbeted posts and uprights

2x4 upright

4x4 post

2x4 bottom rail

4'

6'

2'

2'

8'

Slatted screen
By changing the spacing between the slats, you can adjust the amount of shade and privacy this screen provides.

Canvas screen
Attach the canvas to the frame with screws and grommets; cover the edges with strips of 1-by lumber.

2x4 top rail

2x6 bottom rail

1x2 slat

4x4 post

FINISHING TOUCHES

Many homeowners find themselves confronted with dull, ordinary fences. Or, they may have to face the less attractive side of a neighbor's fence; but these are not unsolvable problems. There are a number of ways to add visual interest to your fence with decoration, plantings, lighting, or finishes, as described on the following pages.

Plants and fences go well together: Without plants around it, a fence can look flat; and without a fence nearby, plants can seem stranded. Plants provide living patterns, textures, and colors that can conceal or soften the stern lines of a fence. Espaliered plants or leafy vines can work with an open-design fence to shade a section of garden from the afternoon sun. A fence can furnish support for vines and planters as well as a backdrop against which to train decorative shrubs.

At night, lights can give a new dimension to a fence and the plantings around it, accenting decorative shrubs. Plants viewed in silhouette against a lighted fence cast an entrancing pattern of shadows on the fence; see page 83 for information on different lighting effects.

Sometimes just a fresh application of paint or stain can give a fence a more interesting look. For information on painting or staining a fence, turn to page 81.

Shrubs or flowers planted near an open fence can beautify both sides.

FENCE DECORATION

A few decorating ideas are presented here; with some thought and creativity, you can adapt them to your fence or come up with unique ideas of your own. Keep in mind that your modifications shouldn't add much weight to your fence, since the structure was designed to carry a specific load. To stand up under the addition of heavy materials, your fence will require additional bracing unless it's exceptionally sturdy. Before you start, be sure to make any repairs necessary to put your fence in first-class condition.

Some pieces of wood and a few saw cuts can spruce up a prosaic fence post. Or you can buy prefabricated fence caps, which can be attached to your existing posts. Choose one of the treatments shown at right, or browse through the color photos in the first chapter of the book for some inspiration. For other ideas, have a look at the fences you pass in your daily travels. You can also add interest to your fence by adding a fence cap —either made at home or purchased where fence materials are sold. Something as simple as adding a piece of 2x6 across the top of the fence *(right, bottom)* can be a big improvement.

The most noticeable part of a fence is the face; you can add a decorative panel to give yours a new look, or cut a window in it for a glimpse of the view. You can fasten a lath lattice on the frame side and train plants up it. A simple checkerboard pattern of vertical and horizontal 2x4s added to the frame side can give your fence a facelift, especially if you place a few plants on it.

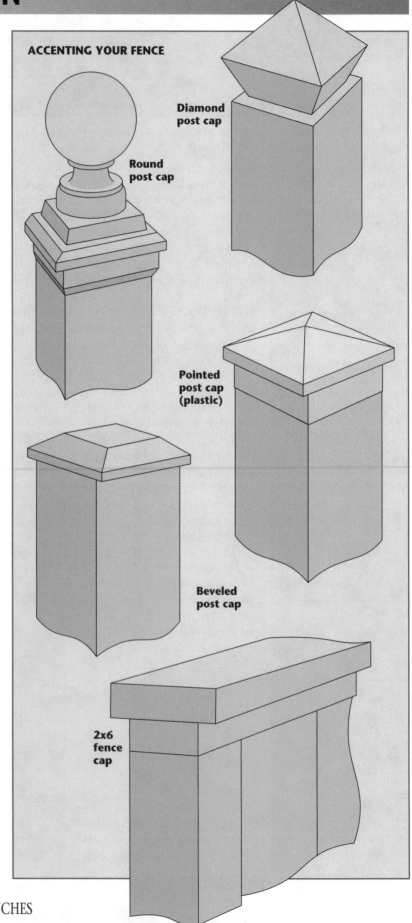

ACCENTING YOUR FENCE

Round post cap

Diamond post cap

Pointed post cap (plastic)

Beveled post cap

2x6 fence cap

FINISHES

In choosing your finish, first consider how you want the fence to look—whether you want to paint the fence, stain it, or let it weather naturally—then consider the ease of application and the durability of each finish.

Paint lasts longer on relatively smooth surfaces like plywood panels, surfaced boards, or metal. But stains are easier to apply on rough wood surfaces.

If you plan to retain the fence's natural wood color, you can use a clear water repellent to extend the life of the wood. But there is nothing that you can do to keep the wood looking new forever; unless painted or stained, all wood fences will eventually weather to a natural gray color. If you find this aged look attractive, you can actually speed up the process by applying a gray stain combined with a bleaching agent—when the stain wears off, the bleaching agent, along with the action of the sun and rain, will have sufficiently weathered the fence.

Paints require more work to apply than other finishes, often need more maintenance, and are more costly. However, they can do some things that clear finishes and stains cannot: They create solid color effects and permit the use of lower grades of lumber in the fence since their opaque quality masks defects.

FINISHING PRODUCTS

Wood finishes can be divided into four categories: clear water repellents; bleaching oils and stains; pigmented stains; and paints and primers.

Resin-based sealers, varnishes, and synthetics that form a clear film on wood surfaces are not recommended for general use on fences. Because they do not form tight bonds, such films may crack and peel from weathering over periods as short as a year. Refinishing demands tedious scraping, sanding, or application of chemical removers.

The same types of wood finishes can be used for both lumber and panels. Plywood is usually finished with an opaque stain or paint; hardboard is usually painted. Unless the material you purchased is already primed, a primer is recommended when you paint.

Clear water repellents: These provide the least protection for the wood, but they're the best type to use to retain the wood's natural look. Also known as water sealers, they add no color to the wood and don't hide the wood grain, but they do offer protection from moisture-related weathering. Some products combine a water repellent and a wood preservative, which offers greater UV protection than a simple wood finish. Whatever type of clear finish you apply, you'll need to add a new coat every six months to two years.

Bleaching oils and stains: These stains, sometimes also called weathering stains, actually shorten the time required for wood to take on a weathered appearance. At the same time, they offer greater protection than water repellents. They're frequently used with cedar, and when you first apply them, they turn the wood gray. Over a period of about six months to a year, they help give the wood a weathered look. You'll still need to apply a water repellent every two or three years to be sure your fence is protected from moisture.

Stains: Rather like thin paint, stains add color and a protective coating to wood. In general, staining works best on rough lumber. The best stains for wood fences resist mildew and decay, and repel water.

Stains are available in a variety of colors, ranging from pale gray through the darkest wood colors; they can be either semitransparent or opaque. To reveal more of the wood's grain, choose a semitransparent stain. Opaque stains obscure the wood grain and produce a more uniform color. Stains penetrate the wood, rather than forming a film over it as paint does, so either type of stain will reveal the texture of the wood.

Both types of stains may be oil-based or water-based. Oil-based stains generally penetrate better than water-based stains, but water-based stains better withstand changes in temperature or moisture level.

You'll need to apply stain to your fence every few years, depending on your wood and your weather.

Paints: For the best possible weather protection, paint your fence. Properly applied, premium-quality paints should last eight years or so under average weather conditions.

A primer should be used on new wood before a top coat of paint is applied. If you tint the primer with a color like that of the top coat, you will get better coverage from the top coat.

As with stains, you have the choice of oil-based or water-based paints and primers. It is a matter of some debate as to whether oil-based or water-based primers are preferable. Generally, you can use either type, although for some types of wood (such as redwood and western red cedar), oil-based primers are recommended. These types of wood tend to "bleed" into the paint, discoloring it, and oil-based primers help to prevent this. However, you can buy stain-blocking water-based primers. Oil-based primers are often recommended in any case, because they penetrate the wood better. But air-quality laws in many states have greatly restricted the use of oil-based primers and paints because they release volatile solvents into the atmosphere as they cure.

You can apply either an oil-based or water-based paint over an oil-based primer, but if you choose a water-based primer, don't use an oil-based paint. It is important that your primer and your top coat are chemically compatible. Be sure that the manufacturer's recommendations apply specifically to the kinds of treatment and finish you are using. Using materials from the same manufacturer is a head start on compatibility, but it is no guarantee; check the labels to be sure.

A premium-quality acrylic water-based paint is usually a good choice for the top coat. It will allow water vapor to travel through the wood and it is more flexible than an oil-based paint; it will give with changes in heat and humidity and be less likely to peel or blister. It is also easier to work with since it can be cleaned up with water.

FINISHING TECHNIQUES

Painting or staining a fence is a fairly easy, but time-consuming job. The key to success is to properly prepare the surface; it must first be clean, dry, and in good condition. If you've used unseasoned (green) wood, let it dry for at least three weeks. For the longest-lasting finish, treat the lumber with a water repellent and apply the primer before erecting the fence, covering all lumber surfaces. Wait two or more days between soaking the wood with water repellent and applying the primer. Once the fence is built, apply the finish (*opposite*).

ASK A PRO

HOW CAN I AVOID PAINT PROBLEMS?
Paint damage has many causes, such as improper surface preparation, careless painting, and use of the wrong paint. Four common paint problems are illustrated at right. Try to determine the cause of a problem, to avoid it next time.

Blistering is caused by water or solvent vapor trapped under the paint. If there's bare wood under the blister, it's the result of moisture escaping from damp wood. If there's paint under it, it's a solvent blister, likely caused by painting in direct sunlight or on wet wood.

Peeling and curling occur when paint is applied over dirty, greasy, or wet wood or over loose paint.

Alligatoring (a checkered pattern of cracks resembling alligator skin) results when the top coat is applied before the bottom coat is dry or when the paints in the bottom and top coats are incompatible.

Wrinkles are caused by careless painting. If paint is applied too thickly, the top surface dries and the paint underneath droops.

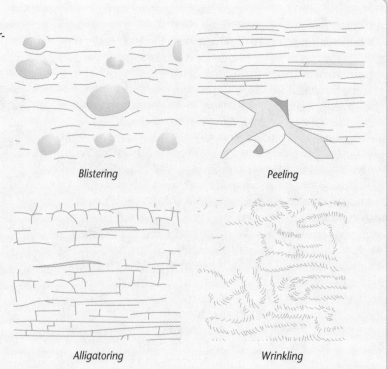

Blistering

Peeling

Alligatoring

Wrinkling

Applying a finish

1 ▶ Choosing your tools

Once you've chosen the paint or stain you'll use, gather the necessary tools and equipment. To brush on paint or stain, use a high-quality 2" brush for narrow strips and tight areas, and a 4" brush for painting wide surfaces. If your fence has wide, flat areas (if it's a panel fence, for example) you can paint it with a roller. Use a roller with a fine nap for smooth surfaces, but one with a thicker nap for heavily textured surfaces; a corner roller works well for tight corners.

You may want to rent a sprayer, some of which are electric, to apply a finish to a fence with large solid areas. Follow the paint manufacturer's directions for spraying. To ensure good adhesion, brush on the primer. It usually takes two coats to get full coverage.

To minimize overspray, use an airless sprayer. Air pressure directed into a holding tank forces paint into a hose leading to the spray nozzle; you pull a trigger to release the paint. The paint is forced out under pressure and atomized by the nozzle into a wide, cone-shaped spray. Since the paint is not mixed with air, it will drift very little. **CAUTION:** An airless sprayer can be very dangerous. At close range, the nozzle pressure is high enough to inject paint under the skin. If you rent an airless sprayer, be sure to follow the instructions carefully and wear safety goggles and a respirator.

2 ▶ Finishing your fence

When you're preparing the fence, and finishing it, protect any nearby plants with plastic or cotton drop cloths; this is especially important if you're spraying.

Because heat may create drying problems and dust, leading to marred or roughened surfaces, try to paint on a cool, windless day. To ensure the paint dries slowly in hot, dry weather, don't paint during the heat of the day. Stop painting before evening dampness sets in.

Brushing on paint or stain usually yields the best results, but you can also use a roller, pad, or sprayer—depending on the surface you're painting. Always start at the top of the fence and work down, painting in the direction of the grain.

If you're using a spray gun, hold it at a right angle to the fence, about 8" to 10" away. To control overspray when painting more open fences, set up a piece of cardboard behind the fence, resting it against a ladder.

LIGHTING YOUR FENCE

A few well-placed lights around your fence can create almost any nighttime mood you want. The terms used by landscape architects and designers for the different types of lighting —uplighting, backlighting, and silhouetting, to name just a few—give an idea of the possibilities.

Uplighting: A single spotlight directed up into a shrub will silhouette some of the leaves and make others seem to glow. The spotlight can be concealed by low vegetation or behind the shrub.

Backlighting: Light is directed away from the plant and toward a fence close behind; the shape of the plant is then seen in relief.

Silhouetting: By placing the source of light close to the planting and directing the light upward from the ground, you can make the shadows appear large and dramatic. A wide-beamed light spreads the light so that interesting shadows appear on the fence while soft light illuminates the plant.

A fence can also make a good stand or backdrop for displaying carvings and other art objects, particularly near entryways and sitting areas; soft lighting directed upward from one side can provide flattering illumination and produce shadows that reveal the object in detail.

You can hire a professional to design your lighting system or you can do it yourself by experimenting with different lighting effects. If you're doing it yourself, be careful: Work only when the weather is fair and the ground is dry underfoot; water and electricity don't mix. To experiment, you'll need a clamp-on lamp or two, extension cords, and flood and spotlight bulbs. Buy bulbs of several wattages so that you can evaluate different lighting levels; in general, lower light levels work better outdoors.

There are many possibilities for lighting your fence. Take the time now to work out the effect you want, and you'll save time and money—and disappointment—later on. But don't let your temporary lighting linger and become permanent. When you're ready to install your outdoor system, call on an electrician for help.

PLANTS AND THE FENCE

A fence or screen can alter the environment of your garden. The nature of the change will depend on the design and orientation of the fence or screen.

For plants to thrive against a fence, they must receive the right amount of sun and shade for their species. But plants that normally need full sun may literally bake when grown against structures facing west or south, especially those painted white or another light color.

One way of avoiding such a heat trap is to allow for air circulation around the plants: Either position them several feet away from the fence or arrange for air circulation through the fence itself by removing a few fence boards near the shrubs.

If the fence runs east to west, the north side will be shady; choose shade-loving plants for that side. The east side of a fence running north to south will be cooler than the west side; it can provide an ideal place for plants that thrive in partial sunlight.

A fence can provide a backdrop for plants; it can provide needed support for vines and espaliers *(page 86)*, and it can support potted plants, either on shelves or hanging from brackets.

A fence can also be camouflaged by plants, so if you prefer not to see your fence, use plants to hide it. Plants can completely obscure a fence or soften its lines so that it blends with the landscape.

YOUR FENCE CAN BE A BACKDROP
Decorative shrubs and plants often appear at their best when displayed against a fence or screen; bold leaves and interesting shapes don't get lost in the surrounding vegetation.

VINES CAN CLIMB A FENCE
Climbing vines quickly adorn new fences and screens with foliage. Though a few will cling to a solid fence (notably Boston and English ivies), most vines require openwork on which to climb, such as a lattice *(below, left)* or a trellis *(below, right)*. Vines that are not climbers must be tied to the fence.

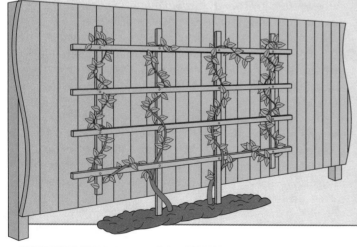
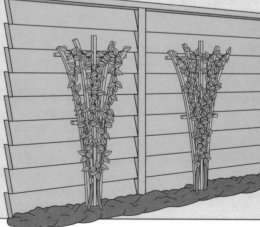

DOUBLE YOUR PLANTS' EFFECT

Plants started on one side of an open fence soon grow through and appear on the other side. In effect, you get double coverage when you plant against picket, rail, wire mesh, or other open types of fences.

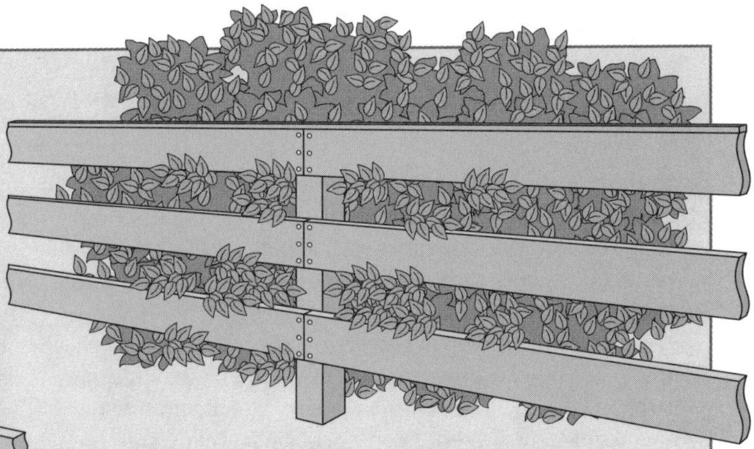

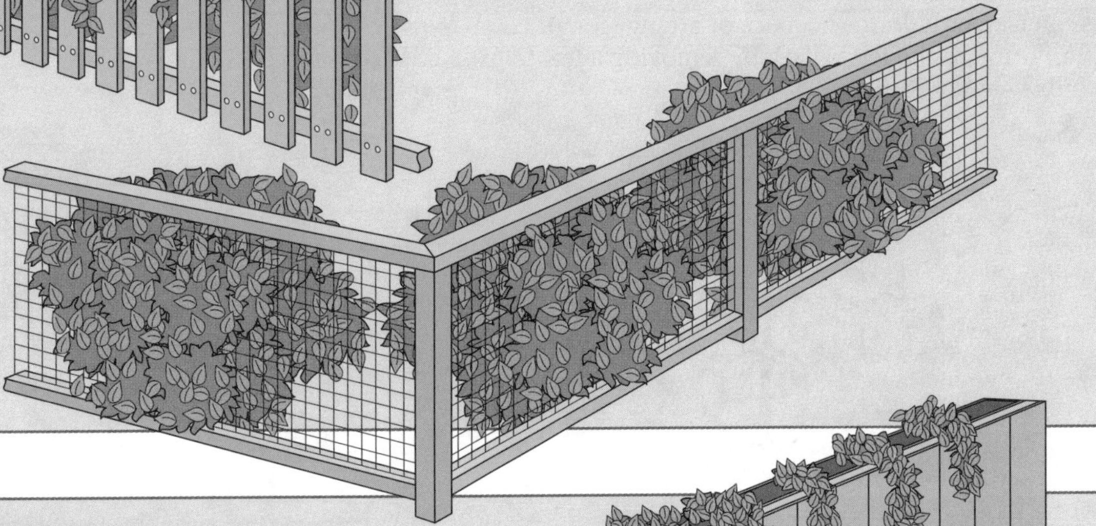

PLANTS ARE AT HOME RIGHT ON A FENCE

You can hang potted plants any number of ways—from the simple brackets shown here to more artistic styles specially designed for your fence. Shelves attached to the fence can support potted plants; the pots can stand free or be set into holes cut into the shelves. Fasten the shelves to the fence with heavy-duty commercial brackets or make your own from wood to match the shelves and the fence. You can also fasten a planter box to the back of the fence and let the plants hang down over the top of the fence.

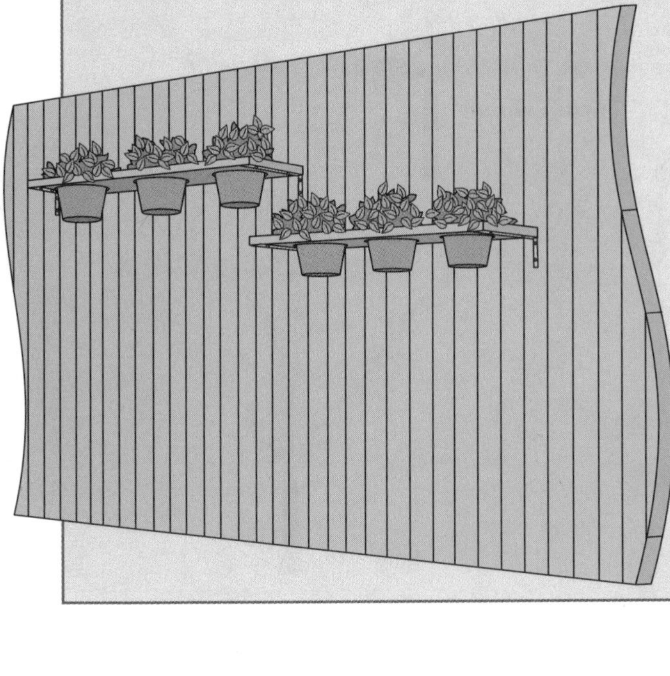

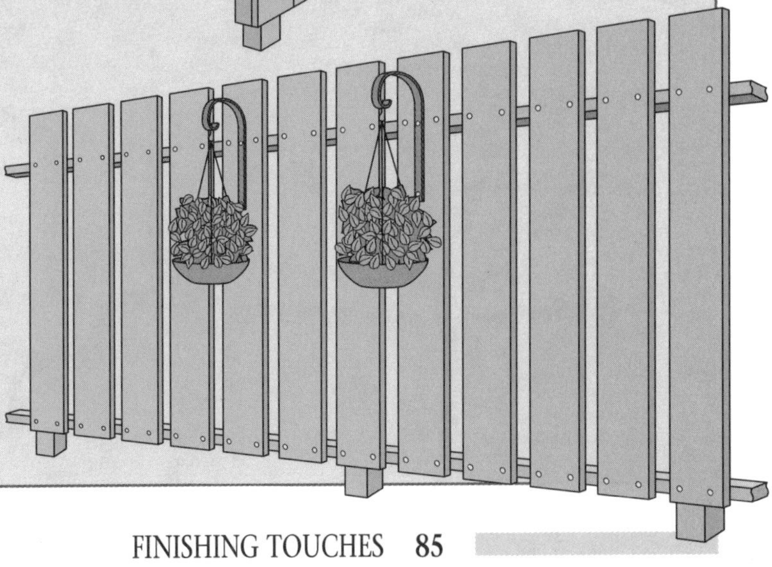

THE ART OF ESPALIER

An espalier is a tree or shrub trained against a trellis, fence, screen, or other support so that its trunk and branches, lying in a flat plane, create an artistic pattern. Placed against a fence or screen, shrubs and trees can be espaliered into shapes that add interest to a bare surface.

Espaliers grow well in narrow planting spaces along a fence, or you can grow them in containers. They require careful pruning, done with an eye for detail and artistic balance. Many nurseries carry espaliers already started and trained by professionals, saving you the trouble of initial training.

To espalier against a fence, you must give a plant support; wire or wood lath, spaced 4 to 6 inches away from the fence, is most often used. The spacing allows air circulation around the plant. Use soft materials such as strips of cloth or plastic plant ties to fasten the plants in place.

As the plantings grow, prune and trim them as necessary to achieve the shape you want.

SOME ESPALIERING INSPIRATION

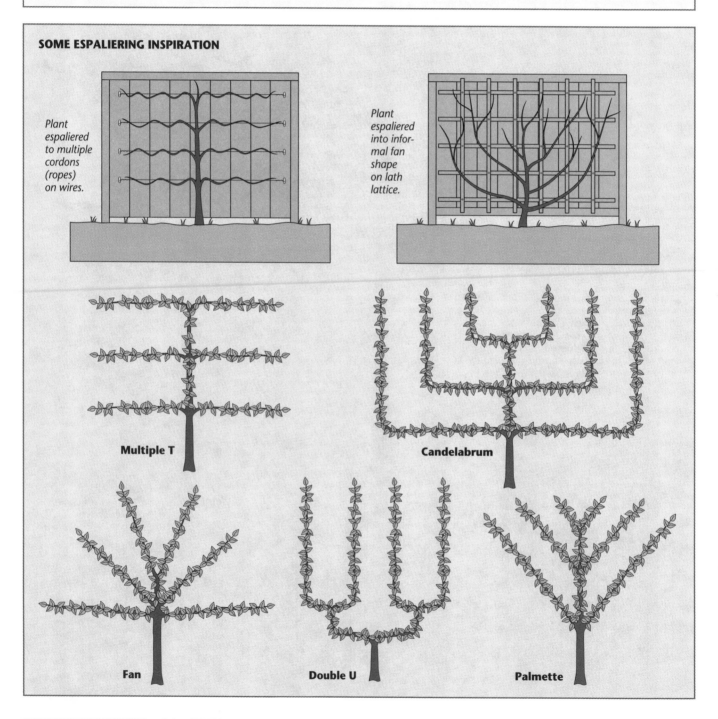

Plant espaliered to multiple cordons (ropes) on wires.

Plant espaliered into informal fan shape on lath lattice.

Multiple T

Candelabrum

Fan

Double U

Palmette

MAINTENANCE AND REPAIR

This chapter focuses on common fence ailments—their causes and cures—and presents tips on keeping your fence in good condition and improving its appearance. Even sturdy, well-built fences require periodic maintenance; fences get damaged, and older ones will show their age. In either case, you can probably do the repair work yourself.

We'll give you tips on periodic maintenance, as well as specific instructions for some common fence repairs, such as repairing a rotted post *(page 89)* and replacing a rail *(page 92)*. Information on gate repairs begins on page 93.

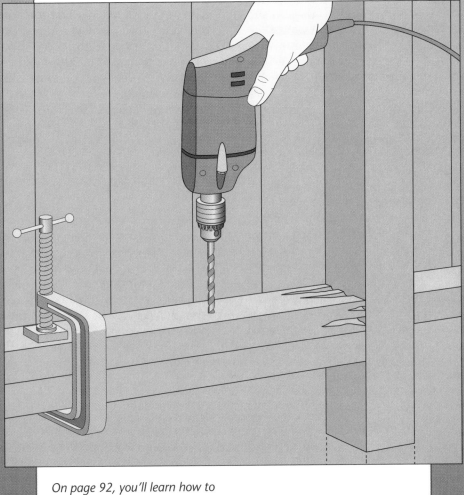

On page 92, you'll learn how to brace a damaged rail by reinforcing it with new, sound lumber.

MAINTAINING FENCES AND GATES

If you want your fence to last a long time, inspect it annually, preferably in the spring while the ground is soft but not too muddy. Check your gate at the same time, since garden and entry gates normally take a severe beating. They're exposed to wind and weather, gate swingers, and people who push against the gate before the latch is free and slam the gate when they leave. Gates that are hung from badly set or insecure posts, or that contract and expand with the weather, often bind, refuse to latch, or scrape along the ground when opened. If you regularly examine your gate and take care of any small problems as soon as you find them, you'll avoid the time and expense of making major repairs later on. But be sure to take care of any problems you notice between annual checks.

Inspecting your fence: First, check the posts for rot. The first signs of decay usually appear on posts at ground level, or a few inches below it. In some cases, the post will be so rotted that a quick visual inspection will tell the whole story. Otherwise, dig around the post about 4 inches below ground level and check it for rot with a pocket knife, an ice pick, or another sharp, pointed tool. If the blade penetrates the wood easily, rot has set in and the post will have to be repaired or replaced.

Check post alignment with a carpenter's level to make sure that all posts are still plumb. Over the years, posts sink or tilt because of unstable soil, frost heaving, or wind action. To remedy the problem, you'll first have to realign the posts, and then reset them; see page 91 for directions.

Next, check for loose rails and siding; drive new nails, if necessary, using good-quality, galvanized nails. If boards or rails have aged to the point where they split when nailed, you'll have to replace them with new ones. If you have plantings against the fence, remove any tendrils or shoots that have worked into the fence; they will eventually pry it apart.

You can extend the life of an unpainted wood fence by coating all above-ground surfaces annually with a water sealer. If the fence is painted or stained, check the condition of the finish; recoat, if necessary.

On metal fences or metal fence parts, use a wire brush to remove flaking paint and remove any rust with a commercial rust remover, then apply a rust-resistant finish.

Maintaining your gate: Because gates are subject to more wear and tear than the fences or walls surrounding them, they'll likely need more frequent refinishing. Wood gates have many joints that can trap decay-causing moisture. Coat unfinished wood annually with clear water sealer; on painted gates, caulk joints and repaint when needed. For more information on finishes, see page 81.

To keep metal gates looking their best, remove flaking paint with a wire brush, use a commercial rust remover if necessary, and refinish with a rust-resistant paint.

Repainting a fence or gate

TOOLKIT
For wood:
• Paint scraper
• Wire brush (optional)
OR
• Sanding block
• Power sander (optional)
OR
• Power washer
OR
• Heat gun and putty knife
For metal:
• Wire brush

Preparing the surface

Before repainting, it is essential to remove any old paint that is peeling, blistering, or flaking; scraping and sanding are the two methods most commonly used by do-it-yourselfers to prepare a wood fence for painting.

Scrape old paint from a wood fence using a paint scraper. Work in the direction of the wood grain, applying moderate pressure. If the paint is very thick, use a wire brush to loosen it.

Paint that is still firmly adhered does not need to be removed, but it should be sanded smooth. You can sand the fence using a sanding block or, to speed up the process, a power sander; wear a dust mask and work gloves. If you use a power sander, you'll still have to work by hand in corners or tight spaces.

For metal fences, use a wire brush to remove flaking paint; steel wool can also come in handy. You may want to use a commercial rust remover to help deal with rust and corrosion.

Two additional tools can help speed up the process of removing old paint from wood: the power washer and the heat gun—and both can be rented. The powerful spray of water from a power washer will remove both flaking paint and dirt; a heat gun blows out hot air, like a high-powered hair dryer, and is useful for stubborn spots. When using a heat gun, wear work gloves and a dust mask. Direct the hot air on the paint to be removed until it begins to blister; this typically takes 5 to 10 seconds. Holding a putty knife held in your other hand, scrape off the loosened paint while moving the heat gun ahead along the grain of the wood.

Once your fence is sanded or scraped, wash it with water and a mild detergent, scrubbing with a stiff brush. Hose off the fence and allow it to dry thoroughly before painting it. Paint the fence as outlined on page 83. For tips on avoiding paint problems, turn to page 82.

REPAIRING A FENCE

Fence repair most often means repairing or replacing posts, simply because they are the most likely fence parts to decay, or to be thrown out of alignment by wind action, unstable soil, or merely the weight they must carry. Misaligned posts can loosen rails and siding materials, causing further damage, such as warping or splitting.

It is best to repair or replace decaying posts before they rot completely through. When a post loses its structural strength because of rot, it not only fails to hold up its share of the fence, but it adds its own weight to the burden that neighboring posts must support. Deterioration of a whole section of fence can proceed rapidly from this point. On the next few pages, we'll tell you how to repair existing posts or replace them with new ones.

Sometimes, the rails or siding need to be replaced or repaired, either because of decay or damage. Instructions for reinforcing a rail, replacing a rail, and replacing siding can all be found on page 92.

Repairing a rotted post

TOOLKIT
- Shovel
- Tape measure
- Sledgehammer or pick (optional)
- Combination square
- Crosscut saw
- Circular saw (optional)
- Electric drill
- Socket wrench
- Carpenter's level

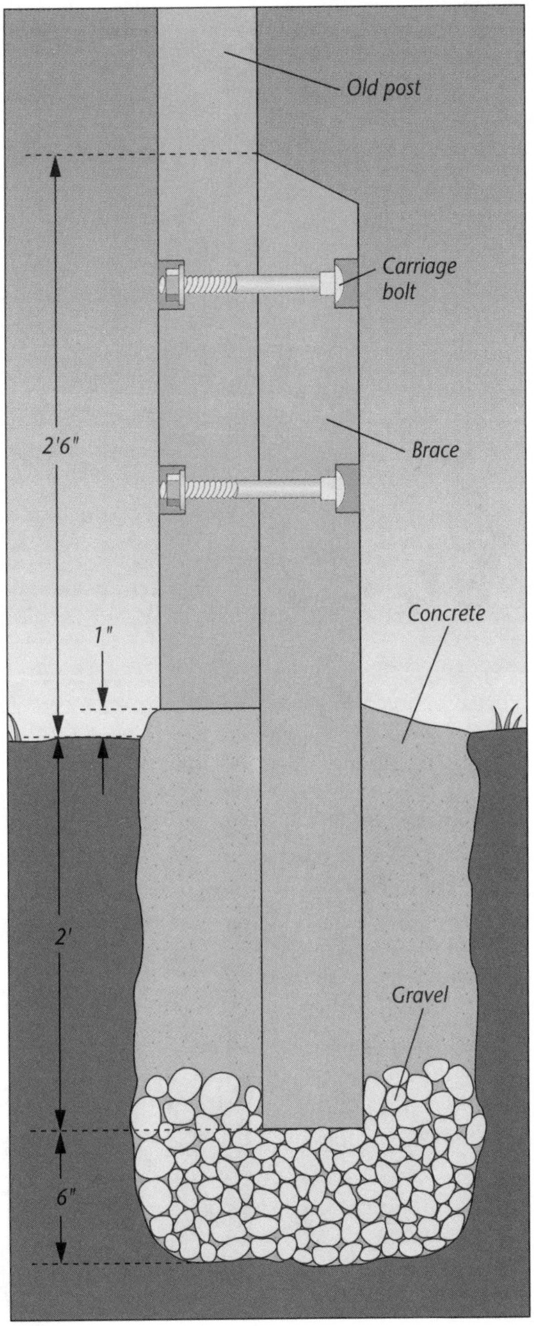

Old post

Carriage bolt

Brace

2'6"

1"

Concrete

2'

Gravel

6"

1 Removing the bottom of the post
When posts are rotted at or below ground level, the repair method described here is the most effective, provided the above-ground portion of the post is still sound. It isn't advisable to replace posts rotted in this manner; removal is difficult, and it's very easy to damage rails and siding while detaching them from the posts.

Start by digging around the rotted post to a depth of 2'6" below ground level. If the post is set in concrete, use a sledgehammer or a pick to break up the concrete and remove it; brace the post and the fence, if necessary.

Cut the post off 1" above ground level and remove all rotted wood from the hole. Do not detach the rails or siding from the post.

2 Installing a brace
Cut a brace about 4'6" long with the same dimensions as the post; use pressure-treated lumber or the heartwood of a decay-resistant species. Cut the top at a 45° angle to allow for water runoff.

Shovel 4" to 6" of rocks or gravel into the hole and set the brace in it, about 2' in the ground. Attach it to the post using 1/2" diameter carriage bolts with nuts and washers; the bolts should be slightly shorter than the combined thickness of the post and brace. While a helper holds the brace vertical, drill clearance holes for the bolts through the post and brace; recess the bolt head and nut, as shown at left. Coat the exposed wood with a water sealer. The bottom bolt should be 6" to 8" above ground level; space the remaining bolts at 6" to 8" intervals.

Fill the hole with concrete (*page 44*), angling the top to allow water runoff. Use a carpenter's level to plumb the post before the concrete sets.

Adding a new post

TOOLKIT
• Tape measure
• Shovel
• Combination square
• Circular saw or crosscut saw
• Carpenter's level
• Claw hammer
For cutting dadoes:
• Chisel and mallet

Installing the post

If most or all of the posts are rotten, or if they're damaged above ground level, install new posts midway between them. This method is also used when the fence design makes repairs on existing posts impractical. For appearance' sake, new posts should be centered midway between existing ones. Do not remove old posts or you'll weaken the fence considerably.

Mark the new post location directly under the bottom rail, centered between two existing posts. Dig a hole 2'6" deep, making sure it's in line with existing posts. Shovel 4" to 6" of rocks or gravel into the hole. Then cut the new post so it can be set 2' deep. If the top rail is set on top of the posts, the new post must butt firmly against the underside of the rail. Otherwise, cut the post to the same length as the existing posts.

If both rails are 2x4s oriented face down (below), cut mating dadoes in both the rails and the post to form interlocking joints when the post is slipped into place. If one of the rails is set edge down (inset), notch only the post where it meets that rail.

Slip the new post in place, setting it in the rocks or gravel in its hole. Check vertical alignment with a carpenter's level and set the post in concrete following the instructions on page 44. Then nail the post to the rails and siding. Recheck the vertical alignment; adjust the post before the concrete sets.

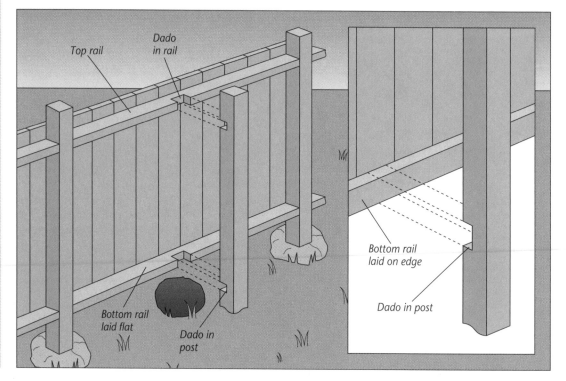

Top rail
Dado in rail
Bottom rail laid on edge
Dado in post
Bottom rail laid flat
Dado in post

Repairing a wind-damaged fence

TOOLKIT
• Tape measure
• Shovel
• Circular saw or crosscut saw
• Carpenter's level
• Claw hammer

Installing a brace

If a prevailing wind has either damaged your fence or pushed posts out of alignment, the fence will need additional bracing after you make repairs so that the problem doesn't recur.

Install a brace cut from lumber of the same dimensions as the post. First, dig a hole about 18" from the post, then cut both ends of the brace at an angle so it sits flush both in its hole and against the post. Plumb the post, then nail the brace against the post on the side of the fence opposite the prevailing wind (right). Set the brace in concrete (page 44).

If the fence is a solid design (panels or boards, for instance), consider making openings in it by removing a few boards or cutting openings in panels to reduce wind pressure against the fence.

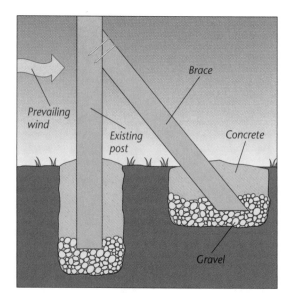

Prevailing wind
Existing post
Brace
Concrete
Gravel

Replacing a post

TOOLKIT
- Crosscut saw
- Prybar or nail claw
- Shovel
- Sledgehammer or pick (optional)
- Claw hammer
- Electric drill (optional)
- Carpenter's level

Installing a new post

Removing a post entirely and replacing it with a new one is the only practical repair method if the fence design would look unattractive with an added or repaired post.

Cut the old post off at ground level and carefully detach the upper part from the rails and siding, using a prybar or a nail claw; take care when removing nails to avoid damaging the rails and siding. Dig out the underground portion of the post, making sure to remove all pieces of rotted wood from the hole. If the post has been set in concrete, use a sledgehammer or a pick to break the concrete into manageable chunks for removal. Dig out the hole to the proper depth *(page 42)* and set the new post in place.

Secure the rails and siding to the new post, using good-quality, galvanized nails; do not drive new nails into existing nail holes. If the rails and siding tend to split easily when nailed, drill pilot holes for the new nails with a bit slightly smaller in diameter than the nail shank. Set the new post in earth-and-gravel fill or concrete *(page 43)*. With a carpenter's level, align the post vertically; brace it temporarily if necessary.

Resetting a sound post

TOOLKIT
- Shovel
- Sledgehammer or pick (optional)
- Claw hammer
- Come-along (optional)
- Carpenter's level

Straightening the post

Wind action, shifting soil, and frost heaving may throw posts out of plumb, causing the fence to lean and also loosening rails and siding. If the posts are sound—no rot is present—they can be realigned and reset in a stronger concrete setting.

Dig out around the post to a depth several inches above its bottom. If the post is set in concrete, break up the concrete with a sledgehammer or a pick and remove the pieces. Push the post into alignment and brace it by driving a stake into the ground and nailing a 2x4 to the post and the stake *(below, left)*. If the post is too hard to push, rent a come-along and use it to pull the post into alignment. To use the device, drive a length of steel pipe into the ground, then attach one end of the come-along to the pipe and the other to the post *(below, right)*; remove siding that is in the way. Crank the handle as many times as necessary until the post is straight.

Plumb the post with a carpenter's level, then shovel concrete into the hole and tamp it firmly. Let the post set for at least 48 hours before removing the brace and reattaching the rails and siding.

2x4 brace

Carpenter's level

Stake

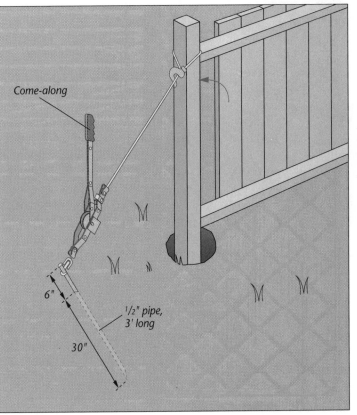

Come-along

6"

1/2" pipe, 3' long

30"

Reinforcing a rail

TOOLKIT
- Circular saw or crosscut saw
- Electric drill
- Screwdriver

To reinforce an entire rail:
- C-clamp
- Wrench
- Claw hammer

Bracing the rail

To reinforce the end of a rail, make a brace from lumber of the same dimensions as the rail, cutting it about the same length as the width of the rail. Hold the brace under the rail, drill pilot holes and screw it to the post. Fasten it to the end of the rail as well, if the rail isn't too rotten.

To reinforce the entire length of the rail, cut a length of lumber of the same dimensions as the rail to fit between the posts under the rail. If there's no room under the rail, install the reinforcing rail on top of it. Hold the rail in place with a C-clamp and drill holes through the two rails, staggered along their entire length, about 18" to 24" apart *(right)*. Install carriage bolts in the holes. Toenail the reinforcing rail to the posts.

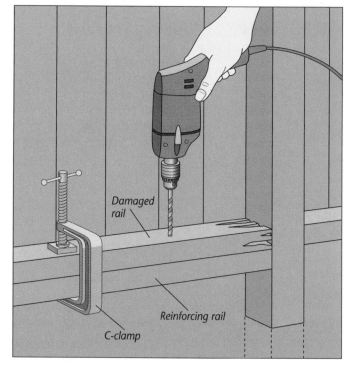

Damaged rail

Reinforcing rail

C-clamp

Repairing a rail

TOOLKIT
- Prybar or nail claw (optional)
- Circular saw
- Crosscut saw
- C-clamp
- Electric drill
- Wrench
- Claw hammer

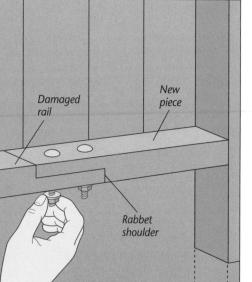

Damaged rail

New piece

Rabbet shoulder

Splicing the rail

To repair a rail, you can remove the damaged section and splice in a new piece using a half-lap joint. Start by removing any siding in the way, then unfasten the damaged end of the rail from the post. If the rail extends past the front of the post, cut it in the middle of the post. Support the rail on blocks, or have a helper hold it, while you cut off the damaged section. Then, using a crosscut saw, cut a rabbet in the end of the old rail.

For the new piece, use lumber of the same dimensions as the old rail. Hold the new piece up between the existing rail and the post, and mark the end of the rail and the rabbet shoulder on the new piece. Saw it to length and cut the rabbet. Clamp the new piece to the rail with a C-clamp and drill holes for carriage bolts through the half-lap joint. Install the bolts *(left)*. Finally, toenail the new piece to the post and then finish it to match the rest of the fence.

Replacing rails or siding

TOOLKIT
- Tape measure
- Prybar or nail claw
- Claw hammer
- Carpenter's square

Installing the new pieces

Carefully measure all dimensions of the original rails or siding, and buy replacements of the same dimensions. Use a prybar or a nail claw to pull off the parts to be replaced and any others that are in the way, but be careful not to damage those you wish to leave in place. Fasten new fence members using galvanized nails; don't drive nails into existing holes. Square new rails to posts before joining them, and make sure new siding is level with existing siding. Replace any undamaged parts you removed.

On unfinished wood fences, the color of the new wood will most likely not match the old. You can give new wood an aged look by applying a bleaching stain, following the procedure described on page 81.

REPAIRING A GATE

Many gates aren't overly strong to begin with and may sag out of shape over time. A gate may start to sag long before it begins binding: Correcting the problem early may save major repairs later. Hinges, posts, or the gate itself may be the cause of the problem. Sometimes there's a quick solution, such as installing a gate spring *(page 34)*. Other times, more substantial work is required. On this and the following page, you'll find tips on adjusting hinges and latches, on resetting leaning gate posts, and on correcting problems with the gate itself.

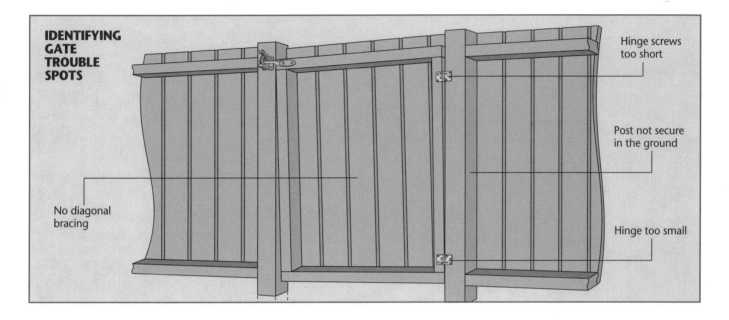

IDENTIFYING GATE TROUBLE SPOTS

Hinge screws too short

Post not secure in the ground

Hinge too small

No diagonal bracing

Solving hinge and latch problems

TOOLKIT
• Screwdriver
• Crosscut saw
• Claw hammer
• Butt chisel
• Wrench (optional)
To shim hinges:
• Electric drill
To reposition lag hinges:
• Pipe wrench (optional)
• Putty knife
• Electric drill

Adjusting gate hardware

Hinge and latch screws often work loose, especially if a gate gets heavy use. This may be normal; but it may indicate that the screws are too short or that the hinges are too small or too few.

To tighten loose screws, remove the screws from the holes. Cut wooden dowels or pegs to fit the screw holes, coat them with glue, and hammer them into the holes. When the glue has dried, trim the dowels flush with the surface using a butt chisel. Replace the hardware, driving the screws into the filled holes.

If the screws come loose again, replace them with the longest possible screws that don't break through the wood on the other side; you can also replace them with bolts and nuts.

If tightening the screws is not enough to make your latch work properly, make any other needed repairs to your gate, such as pulling it back to square or resetting a leaning fence post, before replacing or resetting the latch; see page 58 for instructions on installing a latch.

Loose hinge screws may be a symptom of a gate with inadequate hinges. Gates more than 5' high or more than 3' wide should have three hinges. Two weak hinges can be strengthened with a third one of similar size, placed between the other two and a bit above the midpoint. Better yet, install three new hinges of the largest size that will fit on your gate; use the longest possible screws to attach them.

If the hinge leaves don't contact the gate frame or post properly, insert a shim underneath them. Cut the shim to the same size as the leaves from a piece of scrap wood. Hold the shim and the hinge leaf in position against the post and mark the screw holes on the shim. Drill pilot holes through the shim into the post, then screw the hinge leaf to the post through the shim.

To reposition a lag hinge, first remove the gate by lifting the hinge straps off the lags. Loosen the nut on the lag, if there is one, then remove the lag using a length of pipe or a pipe wrench. Fill the old holes with wood putty. Mark the new position of the lag, then drill a pilot hole and insert the lag. Replace the gate by lifting the hinge straps onto the lags.

Adjusting a tilting post

A leaning hinge-side post is a major cause of trouble. This post carries not only the weight of the gate, but also the weight of anyone swinging on it.

If the post is tilting, you may be able to straighten it up and tamp the soil around it. But this will probably turn out to be a temporary remedy.

If the post is tilting, set it in concrete. Dig around the post to a depth of several inches above its bottom. If it's already set in concrete, break up the concrete with a sledgehammer or a pick and remove the pieces. Realign the post, using a come-along, if required *(page 91)*. Check that the post is vertical with a carpenter's level, then shovel concrete into the hole. Slope the concrete away from the post at the top.

If the post has simply leaned over from the weight of the gate, you can straighten and secure it with a turnbuckle and heavy wire or threaded-steel rod running to the bottom of another post along the fence line *(below)*. This straightening method also works on the latch-side post. You can buy the turnbuckle assembly at a hardware store or home center.

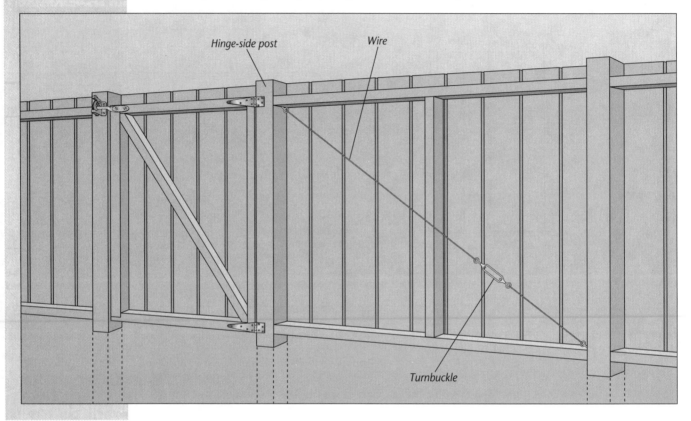

Hinge-side post   *Wire*

Turnbuckle

Fixing the gate

First, tighten or replace loose hinges *(page 93)*. Check the posts and the gate with a carpenter's level and carpenter's square to determine if the sag is caused by a leaning post or is in the gate itself. If the post is leaning, right it *(above)*. If adjusting the hinges or post doesn't solve the problem, the gate itself may be at fault.

A sagging gate with a wire-and-turnbuckle assembly can often be straightened with a few turns of the turnbuckle.

If the gate has a wood brace, square up the frame and renail the brace, frame, and siding. If the gate still sags after you rehang it, add a wire-and-turnbuckle assembly to pull the gate back into place. The wire and turnbuckle should run from the top of the hinge side to the bottom of the latch side; this is opposite to the existing diagonal wood brace.

If the gate binds in wet weather, but works properly when it's dry, plane a little wood off the latch post or the latch side of the gate frame to give at least a 1/4" clearance for expansion. Conversely, if the gate shrinks in dry weather so that the latch will not catch, you will have to either relocate the latch or replace it with one having a longer reach. If the gate has sunk straight down, reset the hinges and the latch.

Baffle
A raised section on top of a fence to direct wind.

Basketweave
A fence design in which thin lengths of siding are woven around a center spacer, either vertically or horizontally.

Batten
A small strip of wood installed to cover a joint or the end of a piece of lumber; protects cut ends from weather.

Benderboard
Thin strips of redwood or cedar, usually about 3" wide and 1/4" thick, used for edging or for making curved rails for fences.

Bleaching stain
A type of stain designed to give wood a weathered appearance more quickly than natural weathering.

Brace
A piece of lumber used to provide either temporary or permanent support.

Cap rail
A board nailed flat along the top rail of a fence; makes the fence more weather-resistant by protecting the siding from exposure to water.

Dado
A rectangular channel cut across the grain of a piece of lumber; used to attach rails and posts together.

Dimension lumber
Lumber 2" to 4" thick, graded for strength, and intended for structural uses.

Easement
A section of property that someone other than the property owner has a right to use. There may be restrictions on how the section is used; for example, if a main water line crosses your property, you may not be allowed to build on or near the line.

Espalier
A form of horticultural training that first flattens a plant against a fence, then coaxes it to assume a decorative shape as it grows.

Frost heaving
Shifting of the ground caused by the alternating freezing and thawing of the soil; can push fence posts out of alignment.

Gate stop
A piece of lumber attached to either the gate post or the gate itself to keep the gate from swinging past the fence.

Grapestake
Rough-split redwood, used as siding for fences; most commonly available in 1x2 slats, but also found as 2" diameter poles. Originally used to prop up grapevines in vineyards.

Half-lap joint
A method of joining fence parts in which one or both boards are rabbeted so that the surfaces of the pieces will be flush; typically used to repair a damaged rail.

Kickboard
A board, usually 2-by lumber, fastened along the bottom of a fence to close the gap under the bottom rail; usually projects underground.

Laminating
Building up larger pieces of wood by gluing or nailing together thin, flexible strips of wood, such as benderboard; to make curved pieces, the strips are bent around a curved form as they are fastened together.

Lapped rails
Rails fastened to the top or sides of the posts; the ends of the rails are butted together at the center of the posts.

Level
Perfectly horizontal; can be determined with a carpenter's level, line level, or water level.

Louvered fence
A design in which boards are set at an angle between rails (vertical) or posts (horizontal), with space left between them; provides privacy but permits air circulation.

Miter cut
A cut that angles across the surface or edge of a piece of wood.

Mortise
A rectangular or round hole in a post sized to accommodate a matching tenon on a rail; a blind mortise passes only partway through the post so that the tenon is hidden.

Nominal size
The dimensions to which lumber is sawn before it is surfaced at the mill; boards (such as 2x4s) are sold according to their nominal size.

Notch
A recess cut into a piece of lumber, such as in a fence post, into which another piece is fitted.

On center
The distance between the centers of two adjacent posts; normally abbreviated o.c.

Paling
A wood stake, usually a peeled sapling between 2" and 12" in diameter, with a pointed top. Smaller sizes are used as fence siding.

Pilot hole
A hole drilled into wood to accommodate a nail shaft or the threaded section of a screw; usually slightly smaller than the diameter of the fastener. The hole guides the fastener and helps prevent the wood from splitting.

Plumb
Perfectly vertical; can be determined with a plumb bob or a carpenter's level used on two adjacent sides.

Post cap
A small board nailed on top of a post to enhance appearance and protect the post from the weather.

Pressure-treated lumber
Wood that has been commercially treated with chemicals to make it resistant to both decay and insects.

Rabbet
A step-like cut in the edge or end of a board; usually forms one half of a half-lap joint.

Rails
Horizontal members of a fence; they may form the main body of the fence, as in a post-and-rail fence, or they may serve as the structural support for siding, as in a board fence.

Screen
Similar to a fence, but does not enclose a space; often installed to provide privacy or act as a windbreak.

Setback distance
The required distance between a fence and property lines, roads, or other boundaries; varies according to local building codes.

Siding
The part of the fence that forms the body or side of the fence, such as pickets, boards, or panels.

Spacer
A piece of scrap lumber sized to ensure the correct spacing between fence parts (such as pickets).

Square
Perpendicular; two fence parts at a 90° angle to each other.

Stake
A small, pointed piece of lumber (usually 2-by) driven into the ground to mark a location or support a brace.

Surfaced size
The actual dimensions of a board after being dried and surfaced at a lumber mill; the surfaced size of a 2x4, for example, is $1^1/2$" x $3^1/2$".

Tempered glass
Glass that has been heat-treated during manufacture to increase its strength and resistance to shattering.

Tenon
The shaped end of a fence part, cut to fit into a mortise.

Turnbuckle
A metal device with hooks or eyes screwed into both ends; it's attached to a wire or cable and turned to adjust the tension of the wire or cable.

Variance
Legal permission to countervene a building code requirement in a specific situation.

Water level
A tool consisting of plastic tubing filled with water for determining elevations of points separated by uneven surfaces, such as from one fence post to another.

INDEX